Dear Reader:

The book you are about to read is the latest bestseller from the St. Martin's True Crime Library, the imprint *The New York Times* calls "the leader in true crime!" Each month, we offer you a fascinating account of the latest, most sensational crime that has captured the national attention. St. Martin's is the publisher of bestselling true crime author and crime journalist Kieran Crowley, who explores the dark, deadly links between a prominent Manhattan surgeon and the disappearance of his wife fifteen years earlier in THE SURGEON'S WIFE. Suzy Spencer's BREAKING POINT guides readers through the tortuous twists and turns in the case of Andrea Yates, the Houston mother who drowned her five young children in the family's bathtub. In Edgar Award–nominated DARK DREAMS, legendary FBI profiler Roy Hazelwood and bestselling crime author Stephen G. Michaud shine light on the inner workings of America's most violent and depraved murderers. In the book you now hold, SUCH GOOD BOYS, veteran reporter Tina Dirmann tells the shocking true story of two brothers accused of killing their mother.

St. Martin's True Crime Library gives you the stories behind the headlines. Our authors take you right to the scene of the crime and into the minds of the most notorious murderers to show you what really makes them tick. St. Martin's True Crime Library paperbacks are better than the most terrifying thriller, because it's all true! The next time you want a crackling good read, make sure it's got the St. Martin's True Crime Library logo on the spine—you'll be up all night!

Charles E. Spicer, Jr.
Executive Editor, St. Martin's True Crime Library

SUCH GOOD BOYS

The True Story of a Mother, Two Sons,
and a Horrifying Murder

Tina Dirmann

St. Martin's Paperbacks

SUCH GOOD BOYS

Copyright © 2005 by Tina Dirmann.

Cover photos of Jason Bautista, Matthew Montejo, and Jane Bautista courtesy Orange County Sheriff's Department. Background photo © Zuma Press.

ISBN: 0-312-99528-8
EAN: 80312-99528-7

Printed in the United States of America

St. Martin's Paperbacks edition / October 2005

St. Martin's Paperbacks are published by St. Martin's Press, 175 Fifth Avenue, New York, NY 10010.

10 9 8 7 6 5 4 3 2 1

ACKNOWLEDGMENTS

I could have never told this story if it weren't for the support and patience of so many people.

To Michael Murray, Andre Spencer, and Craig Johnson—thanks for listening to my never-ending questions, and answering every one.

To Eliza Gano—thanks for all of your research help, and for never saying no.

To *The Press-Enterprise* newspaper and reporter Lisa O'Neill Hill—thanks for the clips and court notes.

And to Sherry Parmet, Daryl Kelley, Kay Salliant, and Ray Locker—thanks for the outlines, for listening to me read (and re-read) endless paragraphs, and for generally listening as I complained out loud.

Finally, to my agent, Jane Dystel, and my editors, Charlie Spicer and Michael Homler—thanks for the opportunity.

"In our society any man who does not weep at his mother's funeral runs the risk of being sentenced to death."

—*The Stranger* by Albert Camus

SUCH
GOOD
BOYS

Peter Martinez was bored, as usual. But after serving twenty-five years in the Marine Corps, including two tours of duty in Vietnam, the retired sergeant major enjoyed the quiet he found as a security guard charged with keeping an eye on the eighty or so multimillion-dollar homes that lined the sandy shore in the private community of Saint Malo Beach in Oceanside, California. He particularly enjoyed working the uneventful graveyard post and had grown accustomed to the simple sounds of the ocean as it roared in the not-too-far distance from his guard shack.

Despite its beauty, Oceanside was a place most visitors zooming down the 5 Freeway simply passed on their way to the more popular destination point of San Diego, just twenty minutes away and home not only to beaches, but to the very popular SeaWorld tourist attraction. In fact, the Oceanside beaches weren't even visible from the freeway, so tourists, and the troublemaking their revelry can sometimes bring, were scant.

Martinez was armed. As a career military man, he'd had a pistol strapped to his side since he was 18 years old. But in the eight years he'd worked as a Saint Malo Beach security guard, he'd never pulled that firearm from his hip.

Still, he stiffened when he saw car headlights break the black night sky just before 2 a.m. on January 14, 2003.

The 2000 Oldsmobile Intrigue stopped several houses away from his shack, but he could still make out two figures as they lifted a bag out of their trunk. He watched as the pair struggled to heave their heavy load over their heads and into the roughly seven-foot-tall Dumpster in front of the neatly kept white two-story home at 2041 South Pacific Street. "Someone's trying to dump a load of garbage," Martinez thought. But this was private property, so he walked toward the car to give them a friendly but stern reminder.

On approach, Martinez saw a tall man, easily over 6 feet, and a smaller man, maybe even a teenager, still gripping their oversized parcel.

"What do you have there?" Martinez asked.

Who knows why Jason Bautista froze in that moment? Maybe it was because he was only 20 years old and still used to listening to adults. Maybe because he was scared out of his mind and wasn't sure what to do.

But he dropped the bag onto the ground and froze. Matthew Montejo, his 15-year-old half-brother, mimicked his every move. Both men looked up at Martinez, who saw what looked like fear on the face of the smaller guy, the one he considered the sidekick.

"We're just dumping some trash," Jason said.

"Well, you can't dump trash here," Martinez said. "You have to pick it back up and leave."

"Sorry," Jason said, before turning to Matthew. "Pick it up, let's get it back in the car."

As he spoke, the old security guard looked down at the bag. He would later tell investigators it looked like a body bag, the kind he'd seen too many times during his years of service in the Marines. In actuality, it was a dark brown sleeping bag and he couldn't see what was inside. But there was something in there. The bag drooped in the middle as the boys heaved on the ends.

Matthew obeyed his older brother's instructions, lifting the bag again. Martinez watched as the folds of the sleeping bag shifted, pulling back just far enough to reveal a human foot.

Martinez felt shock rip through him. His mind reeled as he stared at the dangling foot. He hoped for a moment that he was looking at a doll or part of a mannequin. But the tightness in his gut told him otherwise.

"Hey!" he called out. "Stop! Put the bag down! I want to see what's in there."

Jason didn't listen.

"No," he told the old man as he stuffed the bag back in the trunk and slammed it shut, "I'm not going to let you."

On instinct, Martinez reached for the .357 pistol at his side and pointed it at the men. "I said freeze!" Martinez repeated.

"Fuck you!" Jason spat back. "You're just a security guard! You can't do anything." He slammed the trunk shut before climbing back into the driver's seat.

Martinez stood still, his grip on the gun. But he never fired. There had already been enough violence this night. Instead, as the car sped away, he took note of the license plate number. Returning to his guard shack, Martinez, shaken by what he'd just seen, called the Oceanside Police Department. And suddenly, the calming sounds of the ocean were drowned out by a police dispatcher's voice.

It was about 8:30 a.m. on the morning of January 14 when Orange County Sheriff's Homicide Investigator Andre Spencer peered down the steep ravine off the Ortega

Highway. Earlier that morning, a passenger in a car driving east on the 5 Freeway had spotted what looked like human remains lying in the fields near Mile Marker 79. Spencer was the next one up for an assignment, so it had fallen to him to lead the investigation. After thirteen years as a sworn officer, he was used to dealing with death. But as his eyes strained through a pair of binoculars, scanning the extreme hilly fields down the freeway, he was still startled at the sight, some 170 feet below him, of the headless, handless torso of a white female, clad only in her panties. The remains were ghostly pale because someone had taken the trouble to drain the corpse of most of its blood.

Spencer knew how tough this one would be. "If she had a head or hands," he thought, "we'd run fingerprints, dental records." They'd have to swab the body instead and hope for a DNA match. His mind churned for ideas, determined to find out who this woman was and how she'd met such a gruesome end.

It would be seven days before that license plate number scribbled down by security guard Peter Martinez would hit Spencer's desk—the tip leading investigators to discover that the torso at the bottom of the ravine was 41-year-old Jane Bautista. Bautista, through the course of her life, had become obsessed by the idea that nameless, faceless strangers were out to kill her, but, in the end, her killers would be the only people she ever allowed to be close to her—her sons Jason and Matthew.

When she was a young woman, people described Jane as "striking." Her pale skin covered a thin, 5'7" frame and was set off by long, wavy brilliant red hair. Her soft blue eyes could pierce any man's heart. One neighbor described her as "not flashy, not the kind who wore a lot of make-up or anything. She was plain, but pretty." She probably could have had her choice of men to date, but she fell in love with a simple handyman from Belize. Armando Bautista met Jane while she was a student at the University of Wisconsin–Parkside, where she was taking classes in hopes of someday becoming a teacher. Jane was 19 years old in 1981, the year she returned to Bautista's home in Corozal Town, a lobster-exporting community on the northern coast of Belize, and agreed to marry him. Standing in the pink prom dress she'd borrowed from Armando's sister, she promised to love, honor, and cherish her groom forever.

Armando's family, however, took an immediate dislike to Jane. They thought she was uppity because she insisted Armando rent a hotel room, rejecting his close-knit family's offer to stay with them. Elida Centeno, Armando's mother, was particularly hurt, then enraged, after her son and his wife refused to stay with the family during their visit. But Armando was so eager to please his new bride, he borrowed money from his mom to cover the hotel tab and meals at local restaurants.

By any respect, the marriage was an odd, if not controversial, partnering. Jane came from a very upscale, white, devoutly Christian family. She looked odd next to her poor, immigrant groom. But Jane was always the rebel, neighbors recalled. Her older sister was the quiet one, never causing her parents any trouble. Jane was the one who sparkled, but she had a stubborn streak that kept her at odds with her family, especially her mother, Nellie Osborne.

Jane Marie Osborne had come into the world on December 18, 1961, in a small suburban hospital in Waukegan, Illinois. She was the granddaughter of Benjamin Cloyce Funderburk, founder of Funderburk Builders, a flourishing construction company. It's a company so well respected that local Realtors can expect to fetch a higher price for a home or building if they can advertise it as "Funderburk built." Thanks to her family's wealth, Jane and big sister Deborah, six years her senior, wanted for nothing as they grew up in the security of small-town living. Nellie and Don Osborne dressed their daughters well, sent them to pricey private schools, and treated the family to frequent Mexico vacations when the bitter Illinois winters took their toll. Acapulco was a family favorite.

When Jane was in grade school, her parents moved from their middle-class home in small-town Zion to the even smaller town of Winthrop Harbor, Illinois, where even today the population maxes out at 6,700. Despite her family's wealth and connections in construction, they moved into a simple, single-story brick home with a double-car garage and a sprawling front yard on a half-acre of land. The back yard wasn't enormous, but was certainly big enough to accommodate the family picnic table and a large barbecue. For most of her life, Jane's grandparents would occupy a small house on the neighboring half-acre of land along Russell Avenue.

The town is a fiercely Southern Baptist community where churches outnumber retail stores. Accordingly, it's also a steadfastly conservative and patriotic town. The American flag waves prominently from the front porches of most homes. Even today, the biggest businesses along Sheridan Road, the main stretch in and out of town, is a Veterans of Foreign Wars office and an Outdoorsman shop selling rifles and fishing equipment. A few mom-and-pop restaurants also dot the road, including Gyros-N-Heros, where a Confederate flag hangs over the front stoop and a giant sign reads "Heros Welcome!" Nearby is the competing Stone Creek Grill—owned by the Funderburk clan. The steak and fish restaurant is so well known it draws people from Wisconsin, though that's not a particularly hard feat, since Winthrop Harbor sits against the Wisconsin border. A freshwater marina just outside the restaurant helps bring Wisconsin residents, who crowd the water with boats and yachts in summer months.

"This place ain't nothing but a little jerk town, always has been," says one long-time Winthrop Harbor resident. "We're so small, why, we've tried to get a Target or a Wal-Mart out here for years, but so far, they aren't coming. We aren't worth the effort, I guess."

Jane's father, Don Osborne, chose not to work for the family business, instead making his own living as a dye caster for a local boating company. Finances allowed Nellie the luxury of being a stay-at-home mom. But neighbors said Nellie ran her home more tightly than any office. She was an organized, disciplined woman. "Nellie is very out-spoken and always wants to be the boss," a long-time neighbor and friend of the family said. "I would consider her a good mother, but she was pushy sometimes."

She often ran up against her equally strong-willed daughter, Jane. Frequent fights broke out between mom and daughter, but neighbors and childhood friends recall it was typical teenage stuff—curfew, boys, chores. If it was anything more, locals say, it's unlikely folks would know about it. "Jane's mother cares a great deal about what other people think of her and her family. She isn't one to air her dirty laundry."

As a child, Jane was considered a nice little girl with no problems making friends at school. She was bright, outgo-ing, and the ringleader in playtime activities. She even joined the Girl Scouts, and neighbors still remember what a striking vision she was in the little green uniform that set off her long red mane. But she also evinced a mean stub-born streak, flanked with a quick temper, childhood friends recall. "Once she got mad at you, that was kind of it," a former friend remembers. "She could pull away from you real quick."

She temporarily attended Zion-Benton High School. But when a rash of schoolyard fights broke out, Nellie de-cided to send her daughter off to a private, nondenomina-tional Christian school in Grayslake, Illinois, about a thirty-minute drive from her home. Westlake Christian Academy required two entrance exams to get in—one ac-ademic, the other a series of questions about her faith to ensure that she was a devout Christian. She passed both effortlessly. In fact, for a brief time, Jane was so infatuated by religious teachings, she thought a life devoted to God could be her calling, as her father, Don Osborne, recalled in a rare newspaper interview after his daughter's death. That faith, however, evaporated by the time she entered college. By the time she was in her twenties, she would promise never to own a Bible again.

Her family tried to support her early beliefs and gladly paid out the nearly $1,000 in annual tuition and enrolled her in classes, including theology. She was always an exceptionally bright student, and that didn't change when she took on the rigorous classes and daily chapel attendance offered at the private school.

Neighbor Joyce Yonke met Jane in the tenth grade. The girls took turns spending nights at each other's houses. "Sometimes Jane could be hard to figure out," Joyce remembered. "But there were several of us who hung out together, and Jane was usually just a lot of fun to be with."

At that time in her life, Jane was outgoing and social. She loved going to school basketball games or driving around with friends at night, listening to music. As a teenager in a small town, there wasn't much to do. But the girls made the most of it. Jane seemed happy.

Even among friends, she stood out for her academic performance. "She was a very smart student, and I was sort of average, so we didn't have a lot of classes together," Joyce said. "We had gym and chapel. And we lunched together. But as far as math and science classes, we didn't, because we weren't at the same level. Jane was always in the honors classes, accelerated stuff. But it was a very small school, so you just got to know everybody anyway."

Friends took to calling her "Mother Jane," because of her habit of doling out advice. She had a maturity and wisdom about her that made the other girls trust her. Joyce spent many hours on the phone to Jane, confiding her boy problems, taking comfort in whatever guidance Jane had to offer.

Jane reveled in delving into her friends' problems. Yet, oddly, when it came to herself, she was quiet to the point of being secretive. There was one boy whom Joyce suspected that her pal really liked, but it was hard to tell if they were dating or just friends, and Jane didn't volunteer the information.

She was quieter still when it came to sharing information about her mother, father, sister, or even the grandmother she'd grown to adore.

"That's what made her hard to figure out," Joyce said. "She was always full of advice for you, but I don't even know if she was close to her grandmother or not . . . She really didn't share a lot. She just wasn't very trusting. She always seemed to be looking over her shoulders."

She made straight A's and ended up graduating a year early, ranking fifth in her class, according to school records.

After graduation, in the fall of 1979, she enrolled at the University of Wisconsin–Parkside, about an hour's drive north of Winthrop Harbor. Jane talked about becoming a teacher someday. She especially loved studying languages. She was already nearly fluent in Spanish, thanks, in part, to her family's frequent Acapulco vacations.

But Jane's academic success faltered once she reached college. Her attendance grew sporadic. Ultimately, she attended the university on and off for nearly a decade, from 1979 to 1988, but school records show she never earned a degree. Jane's grandmother said that Nellie had been just three months away from earning a diploma when she dropped out for good.

After high school, Jane's relationship with her mother also took a darker turn. She swore Nellie favored her daughter, Deborah, and Jane deeply resented her mother for it.

Tensions boiled over with Nellie one evening in 1980, when Jane was just 19 years old. Jane decided she needed her mom's car for the night to take friends joy-riding. Nellie was usually generous with the car, letting Jane use it to drive to and from college, or for random nights on the town with friends. But on this night, Nellie said no. She had plans of her own and needed the car. The refusal sent Jane into a rampage. She screamed so loud, for so long, that Nellie was frightened of her own daughter. She reached out, trying to put her arms around Jane and calm her down. But the contact sent Jane over the edge. She balled her fists and threw punches at Nellie's head and stomach. Nellie tried to hold her down. But in the end, Jane beat her so severely that Nellie ended up in the hospital, where she was treated for multiple cuts and bruises. Nellie never called the police on her daughter that night. A private lady, she preferred to deal with the problem inside the family. Likely, cop cars outside the family home would only inspire gossip among her small-town neighbors.

It was the first concrete sign that something was happening to Jane. The normally bright, outgoing, attractive girl was developing a dark side. Her increasingly quick temper pushed people away from her. There was no way of knowing then, but behavior was likely the beginning of a desperate cry for help.

But Jane took solace in the comfort of her grandmother's arms. Charlie Mae Funderburk always lent a sympathetic ear to Jane's complaints about her mother. Even if she didn't always agree with her granddaughter, the soft-spoken elderly woman had a way of calming Jane

like no one else could. Over the years, Jane spent as much
time at her grandparents' house as she did at her own. She
often took on cleaning chores while there, just to help
out. In return, Mae slipped her favorite granddaughter a
little cash. "This is for my girl," she'd say.

3

It was early on in her college career that Jane met the man who would have a profound impact on the rest of her life. She first saw Armando Bautista at a friend's house. He was a local handyman who had recently immigrated to the United States from Belize. Armando wasn't someone a young lady with Jane's background would typically be drawn to. He wasn't educated, and though he was good at fixing electrical things, and therefore often found work, he was broke more often than not. Still, he had come to this country with his sister, both of them in search of a better life. Armando thought he'd found it when Jane Osborne turned her affections his way.

Joyce Yonke said the pairing actually didn't seem that unusual, if you knew Jane's dating history. Despite the very Caucasian community she grew up in, Jane was drawn to men of ethnicity. "The men she would talk about always seemed to be Spanish men," said Joyce. "She seemed to gravitate more towards them than anyone else." And often, the men weren't her intellectual equals. Maybe she preferred it that way, so she could easily dominate the relationship. Or maybe weaker men were the only ones who tolerated her hot temper. Whatever the reason, it was a dating pattern she'd follow for the rest of her life.

Armando and Jane dated for less than a year before

traveling to the north coast of Belize to marry in March 1981 in front of Armando's relatives. Not a single member of Jane's family was there.

"She just wasn't very close to her mother," a neighbor recalled. "And because her older sister Deborah got along so well with Nellie, that seemed to bother Jane. So she wasn't close to her sister, either."

Don Osborne did, however, pick up his youngest daughter and her new husband from the airport in Chicago when they returned. Neighbors were surprised to see Jane suddenly come home married to an uneducated and struggling immigrant. "She could have had her pick of anyone," a neighbor remembers. "She was very brainy and had that pretty red hair. It was odd."

On the outside, Jane seemed happy, eagerly introducing her husband around. So neighbors accepted the couple, and her parents seemed to, also. But it was hardly a blissful union. Problems between the newlyweds began almost immediately.

Despite her family's affluence, Jane found herself in near poverty as a married woman. Her mother and father gave her little to no financial help. But Grandma Mae's soft spot for Jane continued. Just as she'd done when Jane was a child, she would comfort her as an adult. Through tough financial times, Jane turned to her grandmother for financial support—a habit that would last the rest of Jane's life.

Armando struggled to find steady work as a handyman, so the couple moved to Waukegan, just ten miles south of Winthrop Harbor, but, with a population of 90,000, huge compared to tiny Winthrop. Still, Armando's meager stream of odd jobs couldn't keep the couple from landing at Hickory Manor Apartments, a low-income housing complex along Continental Drive made up of drab one- and two-bedroom units.

Jane found a clerical job at a nearby electrical plant, Cherry Electric. But the couple's financial burdens only grew. Eight months into the marriage, Jane found herself pregnant.

On August 25, 1982, in a Waukegan hospital, Jane gave birth to her first son, Jason Victor. It's unclear how Jane felt about what should have been one of the happiest days of her life. Those who knew her then don't remember seeing her much just before and after she gave birth. Many friends from high school had lost touch with her. If there was a baby shower, they hadn't been invited.

Shortly after Jason's birth, Jane finally did reach out to high school friend Joyce Yonke, sharing her baby news. Joyce was now married herself and a stay-at-home mom. So when Jane mentioned she needed someone to watch little Jason while she and Armando worked, Joyce was happy to oblige. But the arrangement only lasted a few days. While in her care, Jason developed a diaper rash. Joyce told Jane she changed him as often as her own baby, who seemed to be doing fine.

"It's okay," Jane told her. "I'm not upset with you at all. I just think it's better if someone else watches him."

Joyce wouldn't hear from Jane again for over a year, when tragedy struck her life.

Jane's joy of becoming a mommy was muted by her mounting marital problems. Before Jason reached his first birthday, Jane left Armando. In August 1983 she packed up her infant son and moved into another low-income apartment in the same town. The young mom rented a two-bedroom unit, which ran about $915. But Jane paid only $27 a month, meaning she was on some form of public assistance. Under local housing programs, the county heavily supplemented monthly rental payments for anyone with a minor child and earnings under the poverty level.

Armando took the failure of his marriage very hard. By all accounts, he became deeply depressed and tried to reconcile many times. Despite their volatile fights, he was convinced he couldn't live without his family—and told Jane so repeatedly. But Jane rebuffed Armando, saying it was over. She didn't love him anymore.

Armando refused to take no for an answer.

On April 3, 1984, Armando paid a visit to Jane and her son. He demanded she come back to him. Despite the money problems, they could work it out, he told her. In her characteristically stubborn manner, Jane ignored her estranged husband's pleas. She refused to take him seriously, and the discussion escalated into a heated argument—then turned into a shoving match. Jane threatened to call the police, telling Armando she could have him deported if she wanted to. It wasn't true, but a frightened Armando fled anyway.

A few days later, Armando would prove to Jane just how desperate a man he had become. Without his wife, without his new son, he was a man with nothing to lose.

The afternoon of April 7, 1984, was uneventful for Jane—she mostly ran errands, her baby boy at her side. It was sometime just before 6 p.m. when Jane and Jason drove west along Sunset Avenue, the road running to her small apartment, which also took her past her office at Cherry Electric. As her car raced by, she noticed Armando's 1975 Chevy Monte Carlo sitting in the parking lot. Why? What business did he have to show up at her workplace like that? Annoyed, Jane stopped to investigate.

She pulled up next to the car, but didn't see Armando. It wasn't until she walked closer, peering into the driver's-side window, that she finally saw her husband, his body slumped to the side and his head resting in the passenger seat. A gaping, bloody wound ran through his chest. She scurried to the passenger door, flinging it open and reaching across to shake him. But as her eyes darted to the floor, she spotted the .357 revolver Armando had used to put a bullet into his own chest. The spent bullet had ripped through his body before lodging deep in the seat's backrest.

Jane ran to the company's security office and frantically reported what had happened. By 6:27 p.m., the parking lot was filled with investigators from the police department and coroner's office. It was hard to tell how long Armando had been dead, but homicide investigators speculated several hours had probably passed.

"Because there was such a large amount of blood in the vehicle," said Waukegan Police Department Lieutenant Mark Stevens, who reviewed the police report filed on the apparent suicide, "the blood had completely soaked through the seats, so he had to have been there for some time."

"And rigor had already set in," noted Lake County Deputy Coroner Jim Wipper. If Armando's body was already stiffening, he had to have been dead at least three hours, Wipper explained.

"In cool weather, it takes about that long for a dead

body to harden," Wipper said. "And April around here, it's pretty cool. So I'd say three hours is a fair estimate."

It was a heartbreaking scene. A man, clearly despondent over the breakup of his marriage, had driven to his wife's workplace and taken his own life. Worse still, not only had the wife found the body, she'd had their little boy with her. Thankfully, Jason was young enough that he'd likely remember none of it.

In Armando's final act of desperation—some might even say cruelty—he left behind a two-page note, blaming his wife for the suicide. "The note was addressed to Jane," Wipper said. "And he tells her, over and over again, that he can't live without her. It's almost rambling, just over and over, in different words, how much he loved her and his son and he can't live without them."

Armando wrote: "I wish you the best and all the happiness in the world to you, to Jason and to all my family and loved ones. My earthly belongings belong to you and Jason. Living without you and Jason is as good as being dead. I've come to terms with myself and the fact that I'll never live happy without you." His mother, still in Belize, would get over his death, he wrote. "Her faith will get her through this." And as for Jason, who would now grow up without a father, well, "Someday he'll understand," Armando says. He notes that his rent has been paid, so there's no need to worry about that. Then he ends with more declarations of love and the fruitlessness of a life without Jane, writing, "You're all I ever wanted."

Anytime someone dies, and nature—heart attack, stroke, etc.—isn't the cause, police launch an investigation. This time was no different, despite the heartbreaking suicide note. Police couldn't ignore the fact that the dead man had been found by his estranged wife. Jane told police of their volatile relationship, culminating in their physical fight just days before. Police briefly wondered: Could the fight have continued today, this time ending in murder? After all, how could a body sit in an open car, in the middle of a crowded parking lot, for several hours, with no one noticing until Jane happened to drive by?

"Reviewing the report," Stevens said, "it sounds strange to me. There's a lot of suspicious things surrounding the death. But in the end, there wasn't anything to link her to a homicide."

Still, there was talk. Neighbors had noticed the same oddities. It didn't matter if authorities had cleared her. It didn't even matter that Armando had left behind a lengthy, poignant suicide note. There was talk.

The shock of it all—Armando's death, finding him, and now the accusing whispers reverberating through the neighborhood—left Jane a nervous wreck.

Out of the blue, Joyce got a call from her old friend just days after Armando's death. Jane was evasive on the details, saying simply that her husband had passed away.

"But she was very shaken," Joyce remembers. Though their conversation was brief, mostly filled with perfunctory details regarding Armando's funeral, Joyce heard the pain in her friend's voice. "I could just tell she was taking his death pretty hard."

Joyce was already pregnant with her second child at the time, battling morning sickness so severe that she skipped the funeral. Anyway, she'd never met Armando. Jane had never introduced him to her, or to any of their high school friends. And now that her husband was gone, Jane pulled away even further from her social circle.

Though she continued to live in Waukegan for several more years, Joyce never again heard from Jane. "I'd bump into a mutual friend here and there and ask if anyone heard from her, but no one did," Joyce said. "She just dropped off the face of the earth."

4

Jane tried to pull it together, holding down a part-time clerical job and sporadically attending classes at the university. She survived financially through extra cash from her grandmother and, since Armando's death, checks from the state. As a surviving minor child, Jason was entitled to his father's Social Security benefits until he turned 18.

Though she had a rocky relationship with Armando's relatives, Jane spent time with his sister, Quiria, still living in Illinois, mostly so the family could stay in touch with Jason. Armando's sister despised Jane, whom she blamed for her brother's death. But to cut her out meant cutting all ties to the only living legacy her brother had. So Quiria tolerated her presence and invited Jane over for dinner on occasion.

As is often the case when people leave their home country, they cling to others who have made the same trek. So Quiria's home was typically filled with immigrants. Among her regular visitors was Jose Montejo and his mother, both natives of Belize. One Friday night in the early spring of 1986, during a small dinner party there, Jose Montejo met Jane. Her pale skin and vibrant hair certainly made her stand out. Montejo, a 24-year-old laborer in a sheet metal factory, couldn't help but stare.

His mother noticed her son's attraction and immediately tried to steer him clear of her.

"Her husband just died," she told Jose. "And everyone is suspicious of her. You stay away from that one, you understand?"

"Everyone told me," Jose remembers, "they said, 'You better watch it with her.' Because everyone accused her of killing her husband. But I didn't pay much attention. I didn't believe that gossip. I'm a grown man. I told my mom I could do what I want."

He also knew that Armando's sister was very bitter over her brother's death and wanted someone to blame. Jane was an easy target. Quiria told anyone who would listen that Armando would never kill himself. And even if he had pulled the trigger, Jane had still killed him. She'd pushed him to the brink of insanity. In her eyes, Jane was a murderer, no matter what. Jose ignored it all. He asked Jane out.

"She could be so much fun," Montejo said. "She could laugh and be funny. We'd just hang out and end up having a good time. If it was warm outside, we'd go to the beach and take Jason. She seemed happy."

And though she was still living in low-income housing and only worked part-time as a receptionist, she never seemed to be hurting for money. Typically, she had more cash than Jose, so she paid for their outings.

"She was such a kindly person then, always very generous," Jose said. "She told me that her family had a lot of money from construction and that her grandmother was helping her out."

Jose had been abusing alcohol for years. But when he met Jane, he cut back on drinking. Then, as he grew closer to her, and especially her little boy, he stopped drinking altogether.

"She did it," Jose said. "She stopped me from drinking because we were happy."

Jose's favorite times with Jane were when they'd all pile onto her little couch and watch TV, just hanging out at home, together.

"We laughed all the time," Jose said. "She wasn't cold-blooded when I met her. But then, you don't know a book until you open it."

Within three months, Jose had moved in with Jason and Jane. He had big plans to marry her one day, maybe have a few kids of their own. But Jane was in no rush. She was on state aid, and if she re-married, she'd lose benefits because she'd have to report his income, Jose said. Anyway, it wasn't long before Jose had his own reason to postpone a wedding announcement.

"She had a temper," he said. "A bad one."

Jose has lived in the United States now for most of his life. But English is clearly his second language. As he remembered back to those first few months when he moved in with Jane, he struggled to find words powerful enough to describe her anger. He paused for thought before finally explaining.

"She could be two different people," he said. "She had one personality, very nice. But then, two seconds later, she was a bat out of hell and I couldn't please her. Then later again, she'd feel sorry for herself and start crying and say, 'Help me, please help me.'"

It seems clear now that Jane was slowly unraveling. But Jose, an immigrant with just a rudimentary understanding of English, probably couldn't see it. She could be great. She could be a terror. She could be pathetic. But he didn't know what to do about it.

At first, Jose thought he'd just underestimated how profoundly her husband's suicide had affected Jane. She forbade Jose, or anyone around her, from ever mentioning Armando's name. But not because she mourned him. "I hate that motherfucker," she'd say. Not even the knowledge that his remains were withering in a cold grave mitigated her loathing.

At times, that loathing became so intense, she lashed out instead at Jose. Jose wasn't always sure what he did to set off her black moods. He could simply be sitting with Jason, playing with the boy or feeding him, when she'd fly into a rampage, accusing him of being "just like him! You're just like fucking Armando!"

Over time, Jose thought he noticed a pattern—whenever he paid attention to Jason, she got mad. Even though Jason wasn't his own, Jose said, he loved the toddler. He looked forward to the times when they could play together. And it enraged Jane. Obviously, she didn't just hate Armando. She hated his son.

"He was just a baby. It wasn't his fault," Jose remembers. "It got so bad, I could just be laying down with him, and she'd start screaming, 'What are you doing? He's not even your son!' "

Sometimes Jose used his slim earnings to buy Jason a toy, or pick him up his favorite meal, a hamburger.

"Why are you doing this?" Jane demanded. "Why are you spending money on him? Don't buy him anything!"

Jane was never the kind of woman to brag about her toddler. Nor was she outwardly affectionate, the kind of mommy who covered her baby with kisses and hugs. But she was a competent caregiver. Jason never went without food, he was clean, he was healthy. Jose tried to fill the gap. Jason, he later remembered, was a nervous, anxious child who had a vulnerability about him, like he was just a heartbeat away from breaking into tears. The most visible sign something was wrong came in the form of constant bed-wetting. Though he was only 3, the incidents embarrassed Jane. And enraged her. Any morning that Jason woke up with soggy sheets meant he'd get a whipping.

"She'd beat his ass so hard," Jose remembers. "She'd have no mercy. She'd beat him with wooden spoons, belts, whatever she could get her hands on."

Worse still were the lashings Jason got if Jane thought he'd touched an inappropriate part of his body.

"Sometimes, when he was real little," Jose said, "well, you know how little boys can be curious about their body parts. And he'd play with his private areas. I remember one time she caught him. She whipped him bad, then tied his little hands up and left him in a corner all day."

Jose readily admits he has a temper of his own. And the worst fights he had with Jane exploded over her treatment of Jason. Back in Belize, Jose's father would come home many nights reeking of alcohol and raring for a fight. If he couldn't find one with a man on the street, he'd turn to his own family to vent his frustrations. Usually, he'd pick on the only sparring partner who couldn't run from him—Jose. Ugly memories flooded Jose's mind as he watched Jane rail against her toddler.

"She reminded me of my dad when she'd get like that," Jose said, "the way he'd beat me. I didn't want to see it. I told her about my dad, but she didn't care."

"It's none of your fucking business how I raise my son," she told Jose.

"Yes it is," he answered. "I live here and I care about Jason."

The relationship unraveled. Jose was not a timid man and his fierce temper was hard to control. He stood up to Jane's rants, screaming back at her, using up every word he knew from his rudimentary grasp of English. When his words ran out, he itched to reach her in the only way he knew how—with physical violence. He'd grown up in a violent world, in the poverty-laden streets of his small Belizian hometown. Using fists to make a point was a way of life. But now, he held back, resisting the urge to strike Jane. He refused to follow in the footsteps of his father. Instead, only months into his new relationship, Jose decided to get out. He turned to his mother, asking if he could stay with her until he found his own place.

But before he could go, Jane found herself pregnant again.

Despite their problems, Jose honestly loved Jane, and he was overjoyed that he would be a father for the first time. So he resolved to stick it out with his hot-tempered girlfriend, no matter what.

"I tried to forget everything me and her went through," Jose said. "We had a baby now and that's what mattered. I wanted to make it work."

He asked Jane to marry him before the baby was born. Jose wanted them to be a legal husband and wife, especially since, though he rarely practiced, he had been brought up in a Catholic household. His mother would never understand having her first grandchild born out of holy wedlock. But Jane was much more practical than her hot-headed and passionate boyfriend. She was still getting Social Security benefits from the state for Jason and was convinced marriage would interrupt that cash flow. So she turned him down.

Matthew Montejo was born on Independence Day of 1987. As fireworks screamed in the skies outside, little Matthew drew his first breaths. Jose was delighted. And even Jane seemed genuinely happy. Maybe it was a sign of good things to come, Jose prayed. Maybe she just needed some joy in her life after all she'd been through. And what could be more joyful than a new baby?

At home, Jane became a doting mother to her new son. She openly kissed his tiny face and cuddled him in a way Jose never saw her behave with Jason. It was heartwarming, until he realized that all the newfound affection was clearly reserved for Matthew only. Jason was still wetting the bed, taking his whippings, and generally being ignored by his mom.

"Jason still got the worst of her anger," said Jose. "She was just mad at him all the time."

The smallest infractions incurred punishment. One afternoon, Jane made lunch for 5-year-old Jason—a sandwich and a tall glass of milk. After, she hopped in the shower while her son ate. At the table, Jason knocked over his milk. It was an accident, but he knew he'd pay. He waited at the table for his mother to emerge. When she did, she glanced at the spilled tumbler and then at her son. She grabbed Jason by the shoulders and spanked him furiously. He screamed until she tossed him into his room. Jason was so frightened of Jane that day, he would remember the incident long into his adult life.

But there were calm periods, when Jane seemed happy. She could be warm and outgoing, planning small family outings and doing the things any mother would do— laundry, cooking, grocery shopping. In the calm after her storms, Jose wanted to talk to Jane about her rage against Armando, and now, Jason. But they were difficult talks. Jane was still an intensely private person, even with the father of her baby. Even after living with her for more than a year, even after Matthew, Jose felt like he barely knew her. He wasn't always sure, for instance, where her money came from, though he assumed it was from her grandmother. And he knew she disliked her own family, but wasn't sure why. She didn't like to talk about them. Ever. Even her schoolwork at the university was a mystery. She kept each college paper in a locked filing cabinet.

"She kept everything from my eyes," said Jose. "I remember there was some patch in that cabinet. Something she said she got from President Reagan. She valued that thing so much. I don't even know what it was for, she wouldn't tell me, but whenever she pulled it out, she'd say, 'Don't ever let me catch you touching this!' "

Jane's soft side came out with increasing rarity. But it was there, Jose said. He saw it enough to stay around. During one such soft moment, Jane finally decided to share the real story surrounding Armando's death. She said no one knew what had really happened that day, not even the police. And she'd been carrying the burden all by herself.

According to Jose, Jane told him how fiercely she'd fought with Armando in the last weeks of his life. Armando had wanted a reconciliation, Jane said. She hadn't. Desperate to get her attention, Armando had told her, "I won't live without you." He wrote her a letter warning her that he was going to buy a gun to kill himself. Jane had even kept the letter all this time, in her little locked filing cabinet, and showed it now to Jose.

Jane said she was actually working a late afternoon shift

at her job at Cherry Electric when Armando drove into the plant's parking lot. According to her story, Armando called her out of the plant to tell her something. They got into his car to talk. Because she was working, Armando was watching Jason and had the baby with him, too. At some point in the conversation, he took out the gun.

"And then he did it," Jose said. "He did it right in front of her face. And in front of Jason, too."

Hysterical, Jane said she ran, taking little Jason with her. She drove home to think for a while before finally returning to the scene and alerting security. She decided to tell them she'd just found him that way, already dead.

"That's why she'd go so crazy whenever she remembered him," Jose reasoned. And it's why she went so crazy on Jason, Jose said. It wasn't his fault, he was too little to have any control over what had happened. But in Jane's mind, it didn't matter. The boy reminded her of Armando, and of that day.

As the time passed, Jane tried to ignore her own mother and father, even though they welcomed visits from their grandchildren. Neighbors remember that once Jane left home, she rarely came back for visits. "On special occasions, birthdays, holidays, or whatever," a neighbor of her parents' remembers, "her older sister always came back, even after she got married and had kids of her own. But not Jane. Jane never seemed to come home."

In a year together, Jose said he only saw Mr. and Mrs. Osborne a total of three times. Even talking about them spun Jane into a violent mood, so Jose avoided the topic.

She blamed her parents for a lot of grief in her life, including her bouts with asthma. Both of them smoked, she told Jose, and that had left her with the breathing disorder.

A main source of tension revolved around Jane's rivalry with her big sister. By all accounts, Deborah was close to Nellie and Don. Unlike when Jane married, when Deborah tied the knot, her parents gave her a house and some land. "The way Jane saw it, she was the smarter one, but it was her sister who got everything. They always helped her and it made Jane pretty jealous."

Jane paid a rare visit to her parents on the afternoon of January 24, 1988. Jose didn't go and he wasn't sure why she decided to see them. But given her contentious relationship with them, it's more likely she went to visit her grandparents next door and her parents were there. She came home in one of the worst moods he'd ever seen.

"I hate my fucking family," she tearfully screamed at Jose, vowing never to see them again. Her tirade scared baby Matthew, who began to cry.

As she spoke, she reached for Matthew, lifting him into the air and then, incomprehensibly, she dropped him. "He fell like a rock," Jose said. "I couldn't believe it." It was probably just an accident, the result of her agitated state. But Jose didn't care. He'd watched her cold treatment of Jason, and suddenly feared she was finally taking her anger out on her littlest son, just six months old.

Jose flew into a rage, grabbing at her shirt so hard, it ripped.

"The next time you do that, I will kick your ass," he told her, and then slapped her, hard, across the face. The pair struggled with each other, with Jose grabbing her by the throat before throwing her on the ground.

Jose stormed into the kitchen in an effort to get away from her, and to calm himself down. But an enraged Jane followed. She flew into the kitchen and grabbed the nearest weapon, a knife.

"You aren't leaving me," she told him, holding tightly to the knife while tears streamed down her face. "I'll kill you before you leave me."

Alarmed neighbors must have heard the screaming and called police, because an officer showed up at Jane's front door, interrupting the argument before it had a chance to escalate any further. Jose didn't deny striking Jane. "I did, and I'm ashamed of that," he said.

Jose landed in jail, according to police records. But a few months later, Jane filed a petition with the Lake County Courthouse in Waukegan to have all battery charges dropped. On May 13, 1988, a judge granted her request.

But the incident was enough to push Jose away. Again, he decided to leave Jane. He packed a few belongings and moved in with relatives. Within days, Jane came looking for him. It was the exact opposite scene from the one she'd experienced with Armando. This time, she was the one asking him to come back. Jose resisted.

"I don't want anything to do with you," he told her. But it was a bluff. He did want to go home with her.

"I realized, I have my little son. I didn't want to abandon the relationship when we have a little baby. I wanted to try everything to make it work out." So he moved home.

Jane became a full-time stay-at-home mom. To make up the difference, Jose threw himself into work to make more money for his newly expanded family. He took on a job as a tire technician, repairing tires for large semitrucks at a company called Palomar Transit. He picked up plenty of overtime, and continued to take on shifts for his old sheet metal employer, too. But he turned every check over to Jane, who claimed she was better with finances.

"I worked sixteen hours a day sometimes, but I never had a penny in my pocket," Jose said. "She always took the check."

It's ironic that as a teenager, Jane had considered herself a religious person, embracing the theology classes she took at Westlake Christian Academy when her fellow rebellious classmates reviled them. But as an adult, she didn't believe in God, once quipping to Jose, "The only God I believe in is the paper with the president's face on it!" Jane said she hated the Bible and wouldn't allow one in the house.

While they were far from living a middle-class life, with the money from Jose's jobs, Jason's Social Security checks, and whatever extra she got from Grandma, the couple did okay financially. Still, there were problems. The next hurdle prompted Jane to withdraw entirely from the town she'd grown up in.

Before Jose met Jane, he'd lived with another girlfriend, Sylvia Correra. Jane even knew her, because she was good friends with Sylvia's brother, according to Jose. After they broke up, Sylvia moved to Texas, where she stayed during most of his relationship with Jane. Sylvia had called Jose several times over the past two years, sometimes even at the apartment he shared with Jane. In the summer of 1988, 24-year-old Sylvia moved back into town. She wanted to re-ignite things with her old flame, Jose recalled.

That summer, Jane found her car pelted with eggs three times. And she received a series of obscene messages on her answering machine. Jose did little to intercede, though he suspected Sylvia was to blame. He didn't think Sylvia would listen to him, he said. So he let Jane fight the battle.

In early August, Sylvia left letters on Jane's car, promising to beat her. Jane had had enough. She filed a restraining order against Sylvia on August 25, 1988, according to court documents. In her handwritten petition, Jane told the court that Sylvia repeatedly harassed her by phone, leaving obscenity-laden messages on her machine, and sent letters filled "with death threats to my family and myself." The order was granted, instructing Sylvia to stay away from Jane, Jason, and Matthew.

But Jane wasn't satisfied.

"A piece of paper isn't going to stop her," she told Jose. "I want to move. And I mean far away, out of state."

She became obsessed with the idea of going somewhere sunny, like Florida. Jose was reluctant, not wanting to leave his job, his family. To ease his transition, Jane suggested a family vacation, just for a week or two. Jose relented, packing up the family and driving them to the Sunshine State.

In Florida, Jane was another person. She was happy again, affectionate. It was the side of Jane that Jose had first met and fallen in love with. She loved trekking down to Florida's white sandy beaches and playing in the ocean with her kids. The only problem was, Jane didn't want to come home. She was enjoying herself and didn't want to go back to real life. So the two-week vacation went on and on. The family went to Orlando, Miami, Pensacola. A month passed, then another. They stayed in hotels, ate at nice restaurants. All the while, Jose worried about the money. He knew his job was lost. But Jane told him to forget about it.

"I have plenty to cover our expenses," she told him.

"How?" he asked. "Where is it all coming from?"

"I said don't worry about it," she repeated. "I have it handled."

Another month passed before Jane agreed to go home.

"We had so many bills piled up at home," Jose remembered. "But thankfully, I got my job back right away, because I work so many hours."

Jane's misery returned almost instantly. This time, she didn't want a vacation. She wanted to move. She decided on another sunny state—California. Specifically, San Diego. Jose didn't understand it. They had no ties to the area, no friends, no family, no jobs waiting. But that's exactly why Jane wanted to go. She wanted to get away from everyone and start over. Remembering how happy she had been in Florida, Jose relented.

"If you really want to do it," Jose told her, "let's not talk about it anymore, let's just go."

At the end of 1988, the family packed all of their belongings into their used Chevy Blazer, and prepared for the long drive from Waukegan to San Diego. Before they hit the road, Jane stopped by to say goodbye to her family. Jane insisted Jose come with her this time, saying she didn't trust her family enough to be alone with them. It was an odd statement. Jose had no idea what she meant. But he silently tagged along as she broke the news to her mom and dad.

The final goodbye was tense, Jose recalled. There were no tears or *I love you*s exchanged between mother and daughter.

"Okay," Nellie told Jane. "Well, goodbye, then."

Despite years of tension, Jane obviously still wanted a loving goodbye from her parents, given her intense reaction to the cold sendoff. Taken aback by her mother's words, Jane retorted, "Fine, to hell with you," and stormed out.

As they returned to their car that day, Jane screamed, "You see, you see! Do you understand now why I don't want anything to do with my family?"

The entire meeting was so strange, Jose had trouble understanding what had just happened. But pressing Jane for more details on why she and her mother hated each other so much usually put her in such a foul mood, she would lash out at him and the kids. So he kept quiet.

"I always suspected there was so much more to that story," he said. "But I'll never know. She wouldn't tell me."

5

The drive to California took three days. Jane and Jose took turns at the wheel, driving day and night.

"She was my co-pilot," Jose said.

Because money was tight, they didn't have much to spend on hotels. Jason, 6 years old, and Matthew, 1, slept in the back seat as the family car sped its way west.

It wasn't an easy trip. The close quarters for so many hours, combined with the fight with her mother, left Jane in a terrible mood.

"Some hitting went on," Jose remembers. "She started hitting me. The anger she had on her family, she took it out on me. And I'd talk back to her, so she'd get so mad, she'd hit me." Jose tried to take it as long as he could. "But eventually, we just started boxing on each other."

Jane calmed down after the family reached California. They stopped at a hotel in San Marcos. It was thirty-five miles from the city of San Diego, but housing there was cheaper, and Jane seemed satisfied. Jose found work almost immediately, once again as a tire technician. Jane found the family a two-bedroom, one-bathroom apartment just off the freeway, and enrolled Jason in the first grade.

But this time, the change of environment didn't have its uplifting effect on Jane. Instead, she grew more odd. She insisted the family eat a strict diet of lettuce and vegetables. "Rabbit food," Jose called it. While Jose and little Jason weren't happy with the diet shift, no one complained. And no one ever asked her why. "If I opened my mouth, we'd start fighting."

Jane's affections for her kids also grew more sharply divided. She had no problem peppering Matthew with kisses or cuddling him when he cried.

But Jason only saw her cold side. Jose had a theory about Jane's affection for Matthew. Not only was he a handsome boy—despite his Hispanic father, he had such pale skin, he looked Caucasian. Matthew looked nothing like his older, darker-skinned brother. Despite her early draw toward Hispanic men, in later years, Jane changed, growing hateful toward other races.

The lack of affection continued to take its toll on Jason. He had always been a smart boy. From his earliest school days, his teachers had pointed that out. But he wasn't very good at making friends. He was quiet, the kind of kid who preferred to sit alone with a toy and entertain himself. Early on in school, he became the target of other boys. As Jose remembers, "He was a little wuss." Sometimes, he'd still have accidents in bed.

Jane was never formally diagnosed with any mental problems. She never saw a psychiatrist, never went to counseling. But throughout Jane's life, people suspected something was wrong with her. Aside from the tough personality and quick temper, Jane just seemed "off," as a neighbor from her teenage years phrased it. Perhaps the possibility that anything was really wrong with her was ignored because she was so bright, academically. True, she never trusted anyone, but people simply labeled her as hard to get along with—not mentally unstable. As her friend Joyce Yonke told one reporter, "Jane was different . . . She seemed paranoid at times and sometimes suspicious."

Jane once told Jose that she took medication for depression, but he never saw her take anything. And he never knew her to see a doctor except when she was pregnant, despite the fact that she had been an asthma sufferer since childhood. Still, Jane was so secretive, Jose wouldn't have been surprised if she did have depression medication hidden away somewhere. Jane was such a smart woman, she surely would have known to seek out help for whatever was making her so deeply unhappy. But even Jane, and probably most doctors, wouldn't have known then that Jane was beyond depressed. She was demonstrating early signs of a mental collapse.

Clinical psychologists know that many mental illnesses don't fully present themselves until early adulthood— sometime between late teens and late twenties. Schizophrenia is one of those late blooming diseases, according to Neil Edwards, MD, a professor with the University of Tennessee Health Science Center who has studied schizophrenia for more than twenty years. Sometimes, he said, there are minor symptoms early on. But people don't recognize them.

"It's like getting the flu," Edwards explained. "For a few days before, you may feel achy, a little hot, tired. Sometimes you have them for a few days and they go away and you think nothing of it. Just a minor cold. But sometimes they persist and develop into the flu. It's only then can you see that tiredness and achy feeling was a precursor to something more serious."

Perhaps it was the same with Jane, Edwards said. Her hot-tempered behavior, her paranoia over not being loved

enough by her parents, by her boyfriends—all signs of a
developing mental illness: paranoid schizophrenia.

"Some people have paranoid personalities, but it never
gets any worse," Edwards said. "But some do. Some develop all the way into paranoid schizophrenia. Then they
hear voices, they think people are after them, famous
people, even. They're delusional. After a while, their stories begin to sound like a complicated novel playing out
inside their heads."

Typically, medication won't entirely stop the delusions. But they can minimize them. Without treatment of
any kind, however, the disease is left to roar out of control. "The disease can get so much worse. Then, often, it
will end tragically," Edwards said. "Very bad things can
happen."

Aside from her sharp temper, there were few clear
signs that something darker was developing inside Jane.
But as her twenties came to a close, her paranoia and temper tantrums escalated. It was only the beginning of the
nightmare to come.

Jose's patience with Jane was coming to an end by the
early 1990s. She was so hostile, any conversation was
tumultuous.

"Only those boys and I know the hell we went through
with her," Jose says of that time.

Jane accused Jose of cheating. She became obsessed
with the idea, routinely rummaging through his dresser
drawers, feeling into his pockets when he came home, demanding to see his wallet. If she just looked long enough,
hard enough, she knew she'd find the scrap of paper
where Jose had scribbled down the number for his latest
whore.

"But she never found anything," Jose said. "So she started inventing numbers. She'd come to me with some number and say, 'Where did this come from?' "

Because of her fixation on phone numbers, Jose was careful not to bring any home. But he had grown close to a male co-worker and the two decided to get together sometime after hours to hang out. Jose jotted down the number, which Jane promptly found. She called the number and was greeted by another woman's voice—the wife of Jose's co-worker. Jane lost control.

"What did I tell you?" she said, gearing up for a fight. She grabbed a knife from the kitchen and whipped open a closet filled with Jose's clothes. She stabbed at them wildly, putting holes in whatever she could, shredding everything.

Exhausted by the years of fighting, Jose decided not to engage. Instead, he packed his things. He was done.

"If you leave me," Jane warned, "I'll call the sheriff's department and tell them you're sexually abusing your son. You'll never see him again!"

It was the worst thing Jane could have said to Jose, and she knew it. Because he'd grown up in an abusive home, he went out of his way to be kind to his own children. Now, to have someone label him as an abuser was more than he could stand.

"If you do, and they put me in jail," he told her, "I will come back from that jail and I will hurt you. Don't ever threaten me with that again."

Jane didn't call the police. Instead, she watched as Jose grabbed a few belongings and left their apartment.

With no money in his pockets, Jose slept in his car that night. Far from his family, without any close friends, and reluctant to go back to Jane, Jose drifted. Deeply depressed, he rarely worked and found himself homeless for weeks. He grabbed meals where he could, even if that meant out of the occasional trash can. At night, if it was warm outside, he slept behind buildings. If not, he slept in his car.

"I had nowhere to go," Jose said. "It's a time I'd rather forget."

By the spring of 1990, Jose pulled himself out of his depression. He got a job as a mechanic and put a security deposit down on an apartment in Escondido, just a few miles away from San Marcos. He didn't want to go too far, hoping he'd be able to at least visit with the boys.

Amazingly, Jane was delighted to hear from Jose again. And she allowed him time with Jason and Matthew. But Jose realized that the visits had become an excuse for Jane to check in on him, ensuring he wasn't involved with another woman.

Jane popped by one afternoon for a surprise visit. Jose was there, in his driveway, working on a strange car. A female neighbor had some car trouble and Jose had offered to take a look. With her sons in the back seat, Jane pulled up to the pair.

"Who is this whore?" she demanded of Jose, right in front of the woman. "Is this your new whore?"

Hoping to avoid trouble, Jose and the woman got into her car and drove off, intent on putting some distance between themselves and Jane. But Jane followed and a high-speed chase ensued. Frantic, Jose's friend headed to the Escondido Police Department. Only then did Jane drive away.

Weeks later, Jane returned. This time, she called first. It was a warm summer day in June 1990. Jane and the boys had spent the afternoon watching the horse races at the

Del Mar Fairgrounds, not far from Jose's apartment. She called from a pay phone announcing they would stop by.

"Matthew wants to see you," she said.

On her way to the front door, Jane spotted a woman leaving Jose's apartment. She let her go by undisturbed and knocked on Jose's door.

"You owe me child support money and I want it all right now," she said. "If not, I'm calling the police and you'll never see the boys again."

He gave her the cash he had on him, but it wasn't enough. She took the opportunity to let her already-simmering temper fly. Jose realized she didn't care about Matt visiting him. Or even the child support money. She was jealous and angry. She stormed into his bedroom, looking for signs that he was sleeping with someone new.

"The next person that sleeps in that bed, I'll kill her!" she screamed. As Jose tried to calm her down, telling her there was no one, she grew more angry, grabbing his brand-new television and smashing it to the ground. She stormed into the kitchen, where she noticed Jose had been cooking a meal for himself and his lady friend. She scooped up the tableware and food on the counter and slammed it all onto the floor. At that, Jose punched Jane in the face. He punched her again. She staggered backward, then gathered herself together enough to leave. On her way out, she grabbed the hand of 4-year-old Matthew, who had been standing by, watching it all.

Days later, Jose got a call from the Escondido Police Department requesting he come to the station for questioning. As Jose would soon learn, Jane had told authorities that her ex-boyfriend had beaten and tried to rape her. At the station, police showed him a picture of Jane's black-and-blue face. Even he was shocked at how bad she looked. He remembered giving her two blows, but she had bruises all over. He was at a loss to explain what had happened.

"I'm not proud of hitting her," he told police. "But she was going crazy in my house, destroying everything, after I worked so hard to start over."

Jane apparently told them she'd received the punches because she refused to have sex with him. The police threatened to charge Jose with attempted rape and child endangerment. Instead, he agreed to plead guilty to felony spousal abuse. According to court records, the deal landed him a year in jail and a $100 fine.

The night before he'd promised to turn himself in, Jose called Jane. He wanted to drop off some presents and hug the boys one last time before going to jail.

"Sure," Jane told him. "Why don't you come over and stay the night? You can sleep with me one last time before you go to jail."

"What?" he said in astonishment. "After you just accused me of trying to rape you? I'm not that stupid."

Jose never saw the boys before going to jail, where he served just 3 months of his 1-year sentence and agreed to 3 years of probation. Days after his release, Jose called Jane to see the boys. He was bitter toward her and it took some time to work up the courage to deal with her again. But after dialing, he found the number disconnected. Weeks later, driving to the apartment they'd once shared, Jose confirmed what he'd suspected after that failed phone call. His family was gone. He knew he should have gone to the police to report his son missing, but given his last interaction with police, he had little reason to believe they would help him. The manager for the San Marcos apartment complex refused to tell Jose if

Jane and the boys had left a forwarding address. Jane had confided in the manager, telling him what Jose had done and claiming to have a restraining order. She added that Jose wasn't even her husband, anyway.

The next time Jose saw Matthew, his little boy was a teenager, his picture flashing across an evening news report announcing that Matthew and Jason had just been arrested for murder.

Looking back, Jose realizes Jane probably needed psychological help. He wonders if watching her first husband take his life was more than she could stand, and she slowly began to lose her mind because of it. But he never saw the worst of it. He was long gone by the time Jane unraveled completely, leaving Matthew, and more pointedly, Jason, to bear the brunt of her insanity alone.

"You never know what's going on behind someone else's four walls," Jose said. "You have to be there, living it, to understand. But I think she just went crazy."

6

What Jose would never know is that Jane had scooped up her boys and moved just a few miles away, to a two-story home in a middle-class neighborhood in San Marcos. Her home on Butterfield Lane was a step up from the modest apartments she'd shared with Jose. The three-bedroom tract home had a fireplace, two bathrooms, a double-car garage and large front and back yards. A little extra cash from her sympathetic grandmother helped Jane afford such a place. Like clockwork, Charlie Mae began sending monthly checks to her granddaughter, between $1,500 and $2,000 each. Jane set up a post office box and directed the payments be sent there. For whatever reason, she was reluctant to give her family her home address. Although Nellie had a strained relationship with her daughter, she still felt sorry for Jane's two boys. So she supported Mae's decision to send financial help. Each month, Nellie sent the checks by certified mail, along with a note: "To whom it may concern, please make sure this check gets to Jane Bautista."

Jane's new San Marcos neighbors remember the pretty, petite single mom who moved in with her two sons back in 1992. Once again, it was her appearance that helped her stand out. Those around her noticed she was always "impeccably made up," in the words of one neighbor. She wore short, stylish skirts, which flattered her thin figure, and kept her hair long and curly. Neighbors assumed by her looks that she was a woman of financial means—especially since she didn't seem to hold down a regular job. Later, Jane, in a rare moment of seeming candor, told a neighbor that her mother and father had disowned her years ago, but she had a very wealthy grandmother who took care of her. Although she was an intensely private person, it seemed important to her that people know she came from an upscale background.

"She was real uppity," remembers neighbor Paula Toedt. "She always had her nose in the air . . . Nothing was good enough for her."

At first, she was reclusive, hard to know, neighbors said. Early on, Paula, living just three houses down from Jane, became one of her few friends on the block. Paula, like Jane, was also newly single, having just gone through a divorce. She had a daughter a few years older than Jason. The pair had dinner at each other's homes. Paula often babysat for Jane, whose dating life had kicked into full gear.

"She had so many guys coming and going from her place, it was impossible to tell who was who," a next-door neighbor said.

Jane relished being a single woman again. Her favorite haunt was the very upscale community of La Jolla, known for its high-end retail shops and oceanside homes with values averaging in the multi-millions. She loved the downtown bars and restaurants, sometimes dragging Paula with her to go dancing for the evening. Her pretty features easily attracted men. Again, Jane was drawn to men of ethnicity. But this time, she went after a string of Arabic men. They tended to have a lot of money, Jane said, and could treat her right.

Jane even enrolled as a student at nearby Palomar

Community College, where she told Paula she was learning to speak Arabic.

"She always wanted to be taken care of," Paula said. "She didn't work, the entire time I knew her, she didn't work, and didn't want to. She just wanted to be around men who could take care of her."

Some of these men took Jane on trips, usually to her favorite hot spot, Las Vegas. Gambling with her date's money became a favorite thrill. And though Jane never outright said so, she hinted that some of her boyfriends paid her rent and gave her spending money.

"It's obvious, the way she was living, the way she dressed," Paula said. "Someone was giving her money."

One man in particular stood out for Jane, Paula remembered. He drifted in and out of her life for over a year. But she spoke very little about him.

"She was a very private person and really hard to get to know," Paula said. "She was just a strange person, right from the beginning."

Though she didn't have many friends on the block, she had a way of drawing attention to herself. The hours she kept, for one, became a huge gossip topic. Typically, she was home most afternoons, but left around 8:30 p.m. nightly, sometimes not coming home until the very early morning hours, if at all. On such outings, she broke from her normally sharp tailored skirts to don short leather ones and fishnet stockings.

"We nicknamed her Trixie," said next-door neighbor Rosemary Webb. "We all thought it was pretty obvious what was going on. And all the while, those boys would be left by themselves."

Neighbors also noticed the way Jane treated her two young sons.

The brothers grew very close during this time. They were quiet, well-behaved children, especially Jason, who by all accounts was shy and introverted. Jane got into the habit of dumping a lot of the parenting responsibility for Matthew on Jason's 10-year-old shoulders.

"You're the man of the house," she could be heard telling Jason. "So you have to take care of your brother."

Just as Jose had noticed before, neighbors realized that Matthew was her favorite. Jane's sharp tongue routinely lashed out at Jason.

"She'd get frustrated just with everyday life and she'd just take it all out on Jason all the time," Paula said.

It wasn't unusual to catch glimpses of Jane dragging Jason into the house by his arm, screaming obscenities at him. "It was obvious she showed blatant favoritism to the younger one," Rosemary said. "I never saw her raise a hand to that one."

Not long after moving to the Butterfield Lane house, Rosemary spotted Jason sitting on the curb outside his home, sobbing. The crying lasted so long, Rosemary grew worried. She thought it was probably a fight with his younger brother, the only real playmate he seemed to have. She crept outside and kneeled beside him.

"Are you okay?" she asked.

"Yes," he said, nodding his tear-stained face.

"Then why are you crying?"

"I can't get inside my house," Jason replied.

She thought he'd locked himself out and Jane must be gone. But as it turned out, Jane was home. He was making Mom mad, he said. So she threw him outside and locked the door. It would be well into nightfall before he was allowed back in.

Looking back, most neighbors agreed that Jason was a

victim of abuse—mental, if not physical. They couldn't remember seeing him with bruises or cuts. Maybe that's why they never called authorities or demanded child welfare officials investigate. Even when Jane's screaming at Jason could be heard throughout the neighborhood, no one interceded. They considered it none of their business. One neighbor said awareness about child abuse wasn't that well known then. Hard to believe, given it was 1992.

"Unfortunately, people kind of kept to themselves where maybe we could have done something," Rosemary said.

Feeding the family also became Jason's responsibility. Jane abandoned her meals of lettuce and other vegetables, finding it easier to pick up fast food for the boys instead. If she didn't feel like running out, it was up to Jason to put dinner together, usually spaghetti. It was filling, it was quick, and it was easy. Paula remembered once finding Jason at the stove, making his usual spaghetti dinner. He was still little, then—no more than 11, she estimates.

"I couldn't imagine my daughter standing at the stove cooking me dinner," Paula told her. "And she's older than Jason! But you couldn't tell [Jane] anything on how to raise her children. She was too stubborn."

Her family was odd, no doubt. But under it all, Paula sensed that her friend loved her sons, in her own way. "You never saw outward affection because she was so self-absorbed," she said. "She didn't give them kisses or ever say how much she loved them. But I think she did love them."

At times, in fact, Jane was an overly concerned parent, especially when it came to her sons' education.

As Jason transitioned into junior high, his mother became obsessed with his academic performance. Friends, teachers, and neighbors who'd known Jason over the years said he was a very bright boy. "Much more so than Matthew," one friend said. "Matthew was the sweet one, more outgoing. But Jason was the one with the brains."

The better he did in school, the more pressure Jane put on Jason to excel. She expected him to bring home straight A's, which he did. And Jane took to showing off her older son's report cards to her friends. Oddly, though, the display came off like it was more about Jane than her son—proof that she was a good mother, after all.

Once, as a freshman in high school, Jason brought home a B in algebra. It didn't matter that the rest of the report card was full of A's. She zeroed in on the less-than-perfect grade. She reached for a large wooden-handled kitchen knife to emphasize her anger. She never touched him with it, though—just like the times she'd waved a knife at Jose. She just liked to jab it menacingly in his direction while yelling.

"You'll never be good enough," she told him, pushing him back onto the bed in his room. Armed with a 100-foot electrical cord, Jane tied her oldest son up and kept him that way for four hours, "tied like a mummy," Jason would say later.

7

Jason first remembers really suspecting that his mother was mentally ill about 1995. Until then, he knew she had a temper. He knew she could be abusive. But he never considered her crazy, not until that summer.

Jason had yet another blow-up with his mom early that year. This time, it was over a pack of cards he'd bought to play a popular children's game called Magic: The Gathering. The cards cost just $1, but Jane was furious to learn her 13-year-old son had made the purchase. He was not supposed to have any money, and the buy proved he had cash stashed away somewhere, without her permission, she reasoned. Incensed, Jane grabbed a belt and snapped it at Jason. The tail end caught him in the eye, causing it to bruise. That was pretty typical behavior. Jason had long ago stopped being shocked at the depths his mother's anger could reach.

That alone wasn't the incident that convinced him his mother was moving closer over the edge of sanity. It was during an out-of-town trip that he saw clearly, for the first time, signs of the illness taking over Jane's mind.

Jane was in high spirits in the summer of 1995 as she drove herself and the boys to Las Vegas, just a six-hour jaunt from San Marcos. Mostly, it turned out to be a great trip. The boys enjoyed running around the famous Vegas strip, checking out the neon sights, even if they were too young to do any gambling. But toward the end of the trip, Jason flipped on the television and saw musician Duncan Sheik performing his hit song "Barely Breathing." Jane stood transfixed before the television. Then she gently pulled her oldest aside to tell him a secret. She said she'd met him, the singer on TV, one night in a bar.

"Now he's out there singing my songs," she told Jason. "Songs that I wrote!"

Jason struggled to understand what his mother was talking about. It made no sense and he knew it. Was she joking? She was honestly trying to tell him she knew Duncan Sheik and he'd ripped off some song she wrote? The idea was ludicrous. But Jane was adamant—Duncan Sheik was getting rich right now off song lyrics he'd stolen from her. "Now he wants to kill me over it," Jane said. Jason didn't know what to make of his mom's rantings, so he ignored her. She was always an odd woman, and now this was some new tangent he didn't care to get into. But she rambled on, refusing to let the idea go.

Over the next months, Jane was frantic to reach Duncan Sheik. She focused her entire life around the belief that music industry executives were spying on her. She stopped going out during the day, convinced that his people wanted her dead. She stopped using cell phones, and refused to let her sons use them, either. Too easily traceable, she said. Only a direct conversation with the singer could set the matter straight. She didn't want money from him, she just wanted to convince him he should not kill her. She spent hours researching the singer, buying his CDs and reading the inside cover sheets up and down. From there, she found his management firm in Boston. This was her best chance to reach him, she thought. So Jane looked up the number and called. Repeatedly. According to Ever

Kipp, an assistant for David Leinheardt Management, Jane's calls started in 1995. She identified herself as Jane Marie.

"I'm an old acquaintance of Duncan's," she told Kipp. "Could you please pass along my phone number?"

Kipp, not knowing if she really was an old friend or not, took down the number. But, of course, Duncan had never heard of Jane. She called several times, but never reached him. Duncan avoided her, she said, because he couldn't admit he'd ripped off her song lyrics. And in retaliation, his army of powerful entertainment executives continued to watch her every move.

Jane's paranoia swelled that year. She had a long list of people who she knew certainly wanted her dead. Her focus grew to encompass entire ethnic groups, particularly Mexicans and Jews. At first, neighbors thought Jane's claims of someone hiding in her back yard, stalking her, were legitimate. Sometimes, strangers would break into her back yard and watch her family, she told people. Well, neighbors reasoned, Jane did go out with an awful lot of strange men. What if one of them turned out to be a really bad guy? What if she had blown off the wrong man and now he was out to get her, maybe even to take her little boys in the process? It was possible. But nobody aside from Jane ever saw a soul.

"Are you going to be okay?" Paula asked one night during a visit to her home. Jane's anxiety seemed so real, Paula couldn't help but worry.

"Yeah, we're going to be fine," she answered.

But Jane found herself so scared so often, she even called the police for help. She told them the same story she had been sharing with neighbors—someone, maybe

even more than one person, was hiding in her back yard.
She saw them, several times. And she was scared what
they'd do to her. She begged the police to help her. But after arriving at her house, and combing through the back
yard, the officers were perplexed. Like the neighbors,
they never could find any indication that anyone had been
there.

In January 1996, Paula planned a skiing trip to Big Bear
Mountains with her daughter and some friends. She invited Jane and the boys to come along. Paula looked forward to the trip to escape stresses at home. For the past
year, she had been dating a co-worker, but the relationship ended at the worst time possible—late November,
just before all the holidays hit. She needed something to
look forward to, and the trip was it.

But as it turned out, the vacation was far from a happy,
carefree excursion. Jane's constant sniping and ridicule
of Jason put a pall on what was supposed to be a fun-filled
holiday break. Again, it fell to Jason to be his brother's
keeper. And any time he failed, Jane let him have it.

The first night up, the group decided to turn in early,
hoping to rise just after the sun and get a full day on the
slopes. Matthew couldn't sleep. He kept talking away,
making jokes, cracking himself up. His giggles made it
hard for the rest of the group to sleep, and Jason knew it.

"Matthew," Jason urged. "Go to sleep! You have to go
to sleep now!"

When he didn't settle down in time, Jane threw on the
lights.

"What is the matter with you?" she asked Jason. "You
know better! You are the man of the house. You are supposed to take care of him!"

"It was sad to see that," Paula said. "Jason just never got to be a kid, because she wouldn't let him."

Matthew could play. Even Jane, with her crazy dating life, was allowed to play. But Jason was the adult, even if he was only 13.

On the slopes the next day, the trip didn't get much better for Jason. None of them—Jason, Jane, or Matthew—had been skiing before. But Matthew took to the sport naturally. He had a small, lithe frame, paired with the natural fearlessness that comes with being a 9-year-old boy. Within a few hours he was bounding down the slopes on his own. Jason, already a painfully insecure teenager, was a chunky kid who had grown almost 6 feet tall. He struggled to maneuver his lumbering frame against the thin skis. He fell a lot. And as any first-time skier knows, learning to stand up again on sticks designed to speed away from you can be even more difficult than the fall itself. After every fall, the entire group had to stop while Jason worked to gain his balance and stand upright on his skis.

In the end, it wouldn't be just Jason suffering that day. It became a painful experience for everyone watching. But it was Jane's reaction, not a lack of patience for Jason's poor skiing ability, that made everyone uncomfortable.

"She scolded him for not getting it," Paula said. "She'd laugh at him for falling down, then she'd scold him for not being coordinated enough or athletic enough. It was embarrassing."

It was especially hard to take since both kids were relatively good boys, very well behaved. Jason hardly said a word. And when he did, it was to Matthew. It was pretty clear that Matthew was aware of the dynamic—if he acted out, his big brother paid the price. It was a great system for Jane, a pathetic one for her boys.

After the weekend, Paula was fairly certain she wanted nothing more to do with Jane. How could you maintain a friendship with someone who could be so cruel to her own children? Then, before the trip was over, Jane had some news to share with her neighbor and friend. She was dating Paula's ex-boyfriend, the one who had just broken up with her a few weeks before.

"I hope you don't mind," Jane said.

"I was shocked," Paula recalls. "We'd only been broken up two months. It hurt me. It really did."

Jane's relationship with her friend's ex ultimately went nowhere, as did most of her dating attempts after Jose. As Matthew would later tell investigators, pausing to snort in disbelief, "My mom with a steady boyfriend? Are you kidding? She hated men."

8

In the months between the fateful Big Bear trip and the spring of 1996, it's not clear what happened to Jane. She didn't have many friends on her block, anyway. And now, her one close friend had decided to pull away, in part because of Jane's cruel behavior toward her son, and in part because she had fallen in love. Paula was in a serious relationship with a man named Brian Tate by then and had no time for Jane's antics. But Jane had become the victim of something even she couldn't explain. She was beyond temperamental. She was paranoid. She was frightened. And her grip on reality slipped away.

"Please help me, you've got to come over and help me," Jane begged Paula one evening in the spring of 1996. Her former friend seemed in such a panic, Paula and Brian were alarmed.

"There's someone in my back yard," she said. "One of those illegals."

San Diego butts up against the Tijuana, Mexico, border. Each year, countless Mexican citizens pour into San Diego County illegally. Most come in search of work, hoping to escape the overwhelming poverty permeating their own country. Every year, government officials staff more and more border patrol agents along the line that separates the United States from Mexico. But it's a never-ending fight.

Still, they come, by the thousands. Now, Jane told her neighbors, at least one of these runaway immigrants lived in her back yard, and she was scared.

Paula and her boyfriend ran to Jane's back yard.

"Right there," Jane said, pointing to a bush. "That's where he's been living. Can't you see? He sleeps under that bush."

They couldn't see a thing. Just a bush sitting atop some dirt and grass. But Jane was so scared, they believed she saw something. They calmed her down, reassured her that at least for now, no one was there, so she was safe.

Jane's calls for help that spring were only beginning. Weeks later, she called Paula's house again, insisting "the illegals are back." Brian was there and Jane begged him to come take a look. By the time he got there, a police officer was already in her back yard, searching the bushes. Again, nothing was found.

"I really believed her," Paula said. "She had me convinced an illegal was living in her back yard."

Jane called countless times over the next few months, always with the same story. Brian ran to her house nearly every time, hoping to catch the nameless, faceless intruder. He never did.

One evening, next-door neighbor Rosemary Webb was startled by a pounding at her door. Rosemary found an irate Jane on her doorstep.

"It's all your fault," she exploded. "If you didn't hire these Mexicans to do your yard work, they wouldn't be living on my roof!"

A shocked Rosemary stood looking at Jane in amazement. She had no idea what her ranting neighbor was talking about. "I just stood there with my mouth open."

Jane took to calling the police again, this time to report

her neighbor for hiring illegal Mexicans to do her yard work. Rosemary was shocked, again, when an officer knocked on her door to investigate. She told him the claims were ridiculous, but the officer already seemed to know that. By now, Jane's calls for help were so frequent, they knew exactly who she was—and what they were dealing with.

"They'd tell me with a grin on their face, 'Could you please stop hiring the Mexicans so they'll stop living on your neighbor's roof?' "

Jane even took to standing in her yard at night and throwing tennis balls at the roof of her home—apparently trying to hit the Mexicans "living there."

At times, Jane called another neighbor and her husband, who was a firefighter. She thought he could use his pull with law enforcement to help her. She called at all hours. During one 3 a.m. call, she said, "I've got a broom and I'm banging on the ceiling, but they won't get off my roof!"

Her calls became so outrageous, her reputation as a smart but moody woman crumbled. Now, Jane was the neighborhood joke.

"Can somebody be that bizarre and not be on drugs?" Rosemary wondered. "Anyway, everyone was laughing at her."

Otherwise, neighbors ignored Jane as much as possible. It's a shame not one of them thought to call social services for help—if not for Jane, then for her sons. But Jane had grown so reclusive, it was hard to say what was happening to the boys living with her. Sometimes, Rosemary could hear her nightly tirades. Their master bedrooms sat side by side, and Jane's booming rants easily drifted into Rosemary's home.

"It was just filthy language," Rosemary said. "Usually about typical mother frustration things, but with her temper, it would be multiplied a thousand times. And it was all the time."

Jason had long grown accustomed to the irrational rantings that accompanied his mother's temper. But even he couldn't understand her behavior.

"Mom, you're crazy, you're acting nuts," he told his mom one evening at the start of another episode. "There's no one up there!"

Jane turned on her oldest, then 15, enraged. She told him he was an idiot, he didn't know what he was talking about.

"They're coming after me, don't you understand?" she screamed.

She kicked him, pushed him, accused him of being against her, and threatened to throw him out of the house for good. Though Jason could have fought back—he now stood nearly 6 feet tall—he never did.

But at least one neighbor told Rosemary it wasn't the boys he was afraid for. "I'm telling you," he said, "one day, her whipping boy is going to get sick of that. One day, he'll take an ax to her."

There were signs all around that Jane couldn't cope with everyday living anymore. Even her front yard told the story. Normally green and well kept, thanks to the mowing skills of her sons, it turned brown that summer and died. One day, Jane and her boys spent the entire day outside laying expensive sod all over the ground. But to flourish, the bottom ground needed to be thoroughly soaked, the weeds pulled. Jane just laid the new sod on the hard, dead ground. Within weeks, the sod was dead, too. Jane told a neighbor that she was trying to redo the lawn so she could get a refund on her security deposit when she moved. She was tired of the Mexicans on her roof and wanted to leave, she said.

"Funny thing was," the neighbor said, "all that sod was more expensive than her security deposit. It just shows you how screwed-up her thinking was."

Shortly afterward, Jane left the neighborhood. She never told anyone goodbye, or where she was going. In typical Jane fashion, she just left.

Jane's dissent into madness intensified after leaving San Marcos. She no longer believed that illegal Mexican immigrants were after her. It had to be someone more sophisticated, because they watched her every move—not just from the roof of her house, or under bushes in her back yard—eyes were on her everywhere she went. It became hard for her to feel comfortable in any one place for too long. She moved constantly, hoping to find peace. The family lived all over Southern California—Escondido, Temecula, Sun City.

"Mom was never happy anywhere we moved," Matthew would later tell his attorney. "She always thought people were stalking her. This person was a child molester or those people were Jews out to get us. It was always something." The pattern continued for so long, Matthew began to lose count of all the places he'd lived. He would later say he'd moved as many as seven times before hitting high school.

In 1998, Jane took an unusually long break from her transient lifestyle after settling into a house in Menifee. Convinced everyone was out to get her, she had few contacts outside of her own sons.

Jason and Matthew were deeply unhappy. But they went along with Jane, silently swallowing their misery, mostly because, despite her screaming fits and erratic behavior, Jane was their mother and they still wanted to believe that she would never do anything that wasn't in the best interests of her family. She'd have periods of lucidity, where everything was fine. She cooked meals, washed laundry, watched TV, and laughed with her sons. It could be like that for months—then, her mind would seem to snap, and the bad guys were after her again. "We didn't know what to think," Matthew would say later. "Until we got a lot older, we just didn't know any better. We thought everybody's mom was like this. We thought it was normal."

In Menifee, Jane tried once again to set up a life for herself and her kids. She rented a mid-sized two-bedroom home, the kind you'd find in any middle-class neighborhood. She even appeared to date again, according to neighbors who remembered seeing her come and go at night, often very stylishly dressed. She even let Matthew play organized sports.

Not that her behavior was entirely normal. Everyone in the neighborhood could hear her screams, her moans, her unintelligible howling. It could be frightening for even a grown person to listen to. She was still clearly paranoid, telling one neighbor not long after they met that she was hearing voices in the vents of her home.

"That woman belonged in a mental institution," said neighbor Dan Cormier, a youth sports coach who met the boys shortly after they moved into his neighborhood. "Every time I saw that woman, she was yelling."

Matthew and Jason seemed very close, Dan noticed. They were together all the time. And they never had friends over. But both boys seemed happy enough. One of their favorite pastimes was playing roller hockey on a side street near their house. The boys even had nets they'd set up for scoring purposes. Jason was usually the goalie, while little Matthew was the shooter. Dan used to coach kids' hockey teams, so he was drawn to the boys as they played. He started coming out to watch them, maybe give them some advice. Matthew, in particular, had a real knack for the sport, Dan recalled.

"He said he wanted to go pro someday," Dan remembered. "I used to play and coach hockey, so I know kids. They were above-average boys, very intelligent, very nice. Just model kids."

Dan was also an avid golfer and was soon helping Matthew master that sport, too. They often played on the greens at the nearby Menifee Lakes golf course. Again, Matthew took to the sport easily. And he loved it. "He was such a gifted athlete," Dan said. "He had a graceful golf swing. He could have played somewhere, one day, maybe on scholarship. It's a shame he never got that chance."

During those games, Dan grew close to Matthew. Jason, too, but he was harder to get to know. He was a quiet guy, preferring to stay in the background mostly. He rarely had anything to say. Dan sensed things were hard at home. He wanted Matthew to confide in him, if there was anything really bad happening. But the subject of his mother clearly made Matt uncomfortable. "He just shied away from talking about his family," Dan said. "He didn't want to talk about it, so I didn't push."

As Dan would learn, the boys only played hockey or golf if their mother was gone. They weren't allowed out of the house usually, except for school. If she caught them out in the streets playing a hockey game, she quickly interrupted.

"She would come home and they would be playing," Dan remembered, "then she'd just start to yell and scream to get in the house. It was pretty ugly. You could see the look on their faces. They didn't want to go inside. But they didn't have a choice. Who comes home and yells at their kids to go inside when they're just out there playing? It was a control thing."

Many of those rants ended with Jane telling the boys they were just like their "good for nothing" fathers, and would grow up to be losers, just like their dads. Years had passed since Armando Bautista had taken his life, but the memory of that day, and the hatred it stirred within Jane, never left her.

Although she developed no close relationships with her neighbors, she stood out to them because of her treatment of her sons.

"She wasn't a friendly person," next-door neighbor Jean Clement said. "She didn't socialize with the neighbors at all." Jean's bedroom window looked directly across at Jane's, about twelve feet away. In the evenings, Jean could hear Jane's bouts of screaming and profanity. She was frightening to listen to, her voice sometimes sounding like a wild animal howling and moaning in frustration. Aware that someday she might have to call the police on Jane, Jean tape-recorded one of her neighbor's tirades. She held the recorder close to her open window, and even though Jane's was shut tight, her screeches, often punctuated with the word "fuck," were captured on tape.

"Oh God, he knows where we've been!" the tape caught Jane's voice saying. "Please, no! You don't have the right to do that to my children!"

Most of the recording was so faint, it was impossible for Jean to understand what her neighbor was so upset about. But she spoke of "idiots" and a "fat, lying weirdo." It was hard to know who she was upset with—sometimes she seemed to be yelling about a stranger, sometimes she seemed to be yelling at someone in the house, probably Jason.

"I'm sick of your fucking lies," she screamed. ". . . Oh, you're a big man . . . You're going to go under because you're a liar and I'm going to make sure!" She sobbed for a long time before starting again. "This is no life . . . This is my house, so just leave! I can't take any more!"

"Shut up!" a deep male voice finally responded. Likely, this was Jason.

"Just stay there, outside, and just get away from here! I don't have no sons. They're rabble-rousers!"

There was more crying and inaudible screaming before Jane's voice is clear again. "You ruin my son and you ruin me? I already have enough problems. I don't need a fucking weirdo trying to kill my sons, stalking me, putting poison in my drink . . . You're just evil!"

"I think you're a fucking bitch!" a male voice responded. It's probably Jason, even though his pattern in the past was to remain passive during her tantrums. Clearly, the 16-year-old had grown weary of his mother's games. His patience was giving out.

"Filthy son of a bitch," Jane continued. "Crazy criminal!"

The male voice said something, but Jean couldn't make it out. Jane, however, responded clearly. "Fucker! You've got to ruin my son and ruin me and my children? Well, when you're underground, you can't do it, motherfucker!"

It's ironic that even in her ranting, Jane was convinced

she was a good mother. "I mind my own business," Jane said. "I take care of my kids and make sure they don't cause any trouble . . ."

Eventually, one of the boys, it's hard to determine which from the poor recording, had had enough. Again, it is likely Jason who finally stood up to her. "Shut up, Mom! That's enough. That's enough!"

But Jane continued to ramble on and on. "Of course, look what they've fucking taken," she screamed. "The fucking front doors, the front of the fucking garage!"

"Mom? Mom!"

In response, Jane laughed faintly. "Oh great, here come the fucking cops," she said. And she shut up.

It's not clear if the cops did visit the house that night, but both boys remember multiple inquiries by the police over the years. Sometimes Jane called them, sometimes the neighbors did after listening to her hysterical rages. But the officers never did anything. Just listened to her stories, labeled her as crazy, then left. They rarely even spoke to the sons living under her care.

Convinced the boys were abused, at least emotionally if not physically, Jean finally placed a call to Child Protection Services. It was the first time anybody had ever tried to alert authorities on behalf of the boys, something that should have been done years before.

Matt later recalled a social worker showing up at the house when he was outside, goofing around with his hockey stick.

"Is your mother home?" she asked.

"Yeah, inside the house," Matt said.

Matt watched the social worker greet his mother at the door. No sooner did the woman identify herself than Jane told her, "Get the fuck off my property." The front door slammed shut, squarely in the social worker's face. Oddly, today the county's Child Protection Services agency has no record of a call to them, or any investigator visiting the Bautista home. In any case, no one ever returned, according to the boys. And both claim they were warned by their mother, who blamed them for the call. "I better not ever see that again," she said.

"She said she would kill us . . . any time we said we were going to call," Matt later told a prosecutor in his mother's murder case. "We were scared of her." So no one ever reached out to social services for help ever again.

It wasn't only Jane's temper that brought her to the attention of her neighbors. They noticed that she always kept her drapes closed, and sometimes covered her windows with tin foil. And there was her erratic schedule. Just like in San Marcos, Jane seemed to be home all day, and went out late at night. But this time, her appointments wouldn't start until the very early morning hours. Neighbors frequently saw her leaving her house at 1 a.m. But Jane, who took such pride in looking good, now appeared overly thin, almost frail, and pale. Her shoulder-length hair, which used to hang in pretty ringlets about her face, now looked unbrushed. She did make an effort to gussy up for her nightly outings, though, donning tight, short skirts and heavy make-up.

Lots of gossip circulated about Jane in those days, including rumors that she was a high-priced call girl who went out every night to earn her keep. Some neighbors said they were concerned—for the kids' sake, of course. Others were just nosey. Whatever the reason, one lady told her neighbors she was going to follow Jane the next time she made her evening rounds. And so, during Jane's

1 a.m. outing, the neighbor tailed her. It's ironic that in all the time Jane thought someone was watching her, the one time someone actually was, she seemed oblivious to the car tracking her all the way to a nearby hotel. The neighbor watched Jane exit her car and walk up to a tall guy. The man simply handed Jane something. The neighbor couldn't make it out entirely, but thought it looked like an envelope. Jane stood talking to the man for a while, standing outside the hotel, before the neighborhood spy decided she had had enough and returned home. No one ever asked Jane about it—no one ever asked Jane about anything—and they left it at that.

It's not clear what, exactly, Jane was up to during those late-night outings. She once told a friend that she just thought it was easier for her to come and go at night because when it was dark out, it was easier to give her stalkers the slip.

Jason remembered that his mother would go out from time to time, mostly in the evenings, but on some afternoons, too. Sometimes she'd be gone for hours. But he never knew where she went, what she did. She now kept her schedule a secret, even from her own sons.

Through it all, Jason kept up decent grades in school. As a freshman at Palomar High School, he made A's and B's. He had lofty goals, telling classmates he was considering law after high school. Or maybe he'd become a doctor. He liked his science classes and he was good at them. He had computer skills, too. What he seemed to falter at was socializing. He wasn't a popular kid. He was too quiet to make many friends. Some kids interpreted his non-social behavior as arrogance. So, even though he was no shrinking violet when it came to stature—he stood over 6 feet tall—school bullies taunted him. He told

Matthew about it, but not his mother. She might just tease him, too. Maybe even kick him. That had become her latest tool for tormenting her eldest: kicking him for being too weak, kicking him for not watching out for his brother, kicking him for acting too much like his dad. She routinely locked him out of the house and began forcing him to sleep in the family garage.

Jason, now firmly muddling his way through puberty, managed to develop a crush on a girl every now and then. Eventually, he mustered up enough courage to ask one out. To even Jason's surprise, she said yes, and he made plans to take a girl out on an actual date. But he quickly canceled after his mother found out. "You're not man enough to have a date," she told him. "Not a wuss like you." She taunted him mercilessly until she convinced him that he wasn't ready for the dating scene.

Oddly, it was Matthew, not Jason, who seethed with anger at his mother during these times. He thought his big brother was weak for not lashing back at her insults, and sometimes told him as much. But Jason rarely talked back to his mother during her rants. He had learned from experience that it usually just made her worse. It was best to ignore her, Jason told Matthew.

Though Matthew had it easier, they both walked on a never-ending bed of eggshells, afraid their next step would cause her to crack. But no matter how hard they tried to be good, to stay out of her way, inevitably, Jane would lose control, sometimes yelling at them both, reminding them of their no-good fathers, sometimes taunting or kicking Jason. Or, at the worst of times, howling with fear about the ghosts out to get her.

9

While Jason tried to lose himself in his studies, Matthew's main passion was sports, especially hockey. He wanted to play on a team. So when he found out about an ice hockey team in the nearby city of Riverside, he begged Jane to let him join. Jane still had periods of lucidity, sometimes lasting months at a time. She was well enough to cook for the boys, wash the laundry, pay the bills, and yes, even sign Matthew up for hockey. Though the rink was about a thirty-minute drive from their Menifee home, Jane still harbored a particular soft spot for her littlest boy. She wanted Matt to be happy. So she agreed to drive him into the neighboring city and sign him up to be a member of the Riverside Jets 1998–1999 team.

Jane arrived unannounced at one of the tryout sessions held at the Riverside ice hockey rink. In the tight-knit, very cliquey community of junior ice hockey, a new arrival would have stood out anyway. But Brad Joplin, the team's manager, and his wife, Nancy, a school teacher, particularly remember Jane's arrival. Her odd appearance caught everyone's eye.

"She looked messy, unkempt," Nancy said. "Like she didn't brush her hair. I'd learn as the year wore on, that was just how she dressed. Her clothes always looked wrinkled, like they came out of the bottom of the hamper.

In fact, she seemed to get worse as the year progressed. She'd show up to the rink looking just terrible."

But it wasn't only her appearance that raised eyebrows. Most juvenile sports teams are broken down into age groups. To ensure that a 15-year-old isn't playing against a 9-year-old, parents have to provide a birth certificate to prove their kid is in the right age group. Jane bristled at the request. Claiming it was an invasion of privacy, she screamed at the volunteer parents running sign-ups. It instantly earned her a reputation.

"Other parents thought she was weird," Nancy said. "They called her a bitch."

Eventually Jane relented and Matt was on the team for the 1998 season. He played forward center, considered the hardest-working position on the ice. Matt proved to be a solid player because he was adept at offense and defense. And it was Matt who took on the face-off at the beginning of a quarter when the puck is first dropped onto the ice. Team members so relied on his play that the coaches broke the rules for him and let him play in games even if he missed practices. And he missed a lot of practices, mostly because of his mother's erratic behavior. She'd disappear for long periods and nobody from the team could reach her. Only Brad and Nancy had her phone number, which she gave them under strict instructions "to give the number to no one," Nancy said. "Not to other parents, not to other coaches, no one." But when Brad or Nancy left messages, she rarely returned their calls.

"Over the year, she gave us a few different numbers," Nancy said. "She kept changing them, saying the wrong person got ahold of her number, so she'd change it. It made getting ahold of her almost impossible."

Nancy remembers Jane once calling back after a long period of absence. "I only have a few minutes," she whispered to Nancy, sounding very upset. "I'm calling from a pay phone." About a minute later, she hung up abruptly.

Unlike most of the other parents, who resented Jane for her odd and reclusive behavior, Nancy and Brad felt sorry for her. They chalked up her behavior to being a single, overprotective mother who was desperately lonely. They even theorized that maybe she was an abused wife on the run from a brutal husband. Anyway, the Joplins appreciated the way Jane came to practices with Matt—even bringing Jason along every time. She may be different, but she looked like a good mom, they thought. So they reached out to her, inviting her to lunch after practices and chatting with her during down time from the ice. It was the closest Jane had let anyone get to her since living in San Marcos.

In a rare move, Jane opened up to them about her past relationships. She told them how her first husband, Armando, had killed himself, leaving her stranded to raise their little boy on her own. As for Matt's dad, she changed the story quite a bit. "She told us he just wasn't the marrying kind," Nancy said. "And that he never wanted a thing to do with Matt. So one day, she said, she just came home and he was gone. He left her and she never saw him again."

But it was hard to get a read on her. At times, she insisted she was barely getting by financially. After each game, the parents typically took the boys out for pizza. It was hard convincing Jane to let the boys go, but often, they joined. Jane, however, would refuse to eat anything because she couldn't afford it. Instead, she'd sip Diet

Coke. She also talked about struggling to pay rent and utilities.

"Other times, she'd imply she was independently wealthy," Brad said. "She said she had a lot of money stashed somewhere, but she could access it whenever she needed to."

They suspected she did actually have money, since ice hockey is not a cheap sport to play. Equipment, including jerseys, hockey skates, and sticks, ran as much as $800 a season. Plus, each team member had to pay $150 in monthly dues.

Four months into their relationship with Jane, the Joplins were in need of a new car to replace their old 1967 Bug. During one practice, Brad mentioned he was looking at a used Cadillac, but he didn't think he could afford the old luxury car's $4,000 price tag.

"I really didn't have the money to buy it," Brad said. "So Jane just offered to lend me the money. She just said she could. We were just blown out of the water by that."

The woman who sometimes complained of not having pizza money now suddenly had enough funds to pay cash for a used car. Who knows if she ever actually had that kind of money on hand, or if she was just grandstanding for her new friends? But after going with Brad to look the car over, Jane changed her mind. "She wasn't sure it was going to be a good enough car for me for the price, so she passed on it," he said.

Despite their mother's oddities, Matt and Jason seemed like great boys. Jason typically sat in the stands as his brother practiced, usually dragging a stack of books to the top of the rink to do homework or get lost in reading. He rarely spoke, unless spoken to. But most of the adults were impressed by him. "His conversation was very adult," Brad said. "He was obviously a very intelligent boy, very studious. But not a dorky kid, either. Not like that. He could be pretty charming."

Matt was the polar opposite. He was outgoing, and genuinely liked by his teammates. "It's one of the reasons we didn't think there was anything wrong," Brad remembered. "Matt seemed like such a regular kid!"

In the early season, Matt's teammates regularly asked him to spend the night or hang out off the ice. But Jane always said no. Even when Brad and Nancy's own boys, Keil, 10, and Daniel, 12, extended the invitation, still Jane said no. It became obvious to onlookers that Jane didn't like to have either of her boys out of her sight for very long. So the invitations to Matt tapered off. Only once did Jane ever leave Matt to practice alone with his friends. She was gone just briefly, taking Jason to pick up some fast food, then returning to her lookout post. "That was the only time she ever left him alone," Nancy said.

By all accounts, Matt and Jason were close brothers—a closeness probably forced on them because they couldn't form friendships like other boys their age do. During down times from the ice, Matt often sat with his brother to play a fantasy card game called Magic: The Gathering. The Joplins' boys sometimes joined in and talked about how good Matt and Jason were at the game. "We thought, of course," Brad said, "it's probably how they passed time when they were at home, because they couldn't ever go out!"

As the season wore on, Jane's appearance took a dramatic turn for the worse. "She looked tired all the time," Nancy said. "And she was so very pale, so white. She looked sick. And very, very thin."

Her behavior became more erratic, too. Concerned, Brad and Nancy talked Jane into a lunch after practice one afternoon. Over the meal, she told them a story that left them more baffled by her than ever. It was the first time they'd seen the real demons dancing in Jane Bautista's head.

"She started out telling us things were really bad because of some business deal," Brad said. "She had some deal that went wrong and now some people were trying to get back at her."

"Very powerful people in the entertainment industry," Jane said, implying it was somebody in the music business. "And you wouldn't believe what these people can do."

The entertainment people watched her all the time, she said. So she had to move a lot, change her numbers often. And she always kept her drapes at home drawn tight.

"It was so weird," Nancy said. "We talked about it all the way home." Nancy, as a school teacher, was used to reporting abusive or unstable parents to authorities. She knew what to do and took that responsibility very seriously. But she didn't know what to make of Jane Bautista.

"Her story sounded crazy, but she was so sincere about it, so convincing, you almost believed her," Brad noted. And her kids seemed happy, well-fed, clean. The couple decided to just keep an eye on Jane by continuing to befriend her as much as she'd let them.

Near the end of the season, Jane sat with the Joplins during an after-game pizza party. She looked terrible, messy hair, wrinkled dirty clothes. The Joplins took the time to grill Jane about the people she thought were after her. They couldn't believe it was true, but her conviction made them think something was happening to her. They

were desperate to find out what, for Jane's sake as well as
her sons'.

"Who are these people, Jane?" Brad implored. "Tell us
who's doing this to you. Maybe we can help."

"Well," she said, glancing down at his shirt. "Let me
just say, you're wearing his clothes."

Brad looked down at the Ralph Lauren polo shirt he
was wearing, then back at Jane. At a loss for words, all he
could say was, "Really?"

"I didn't know what to think of that kind of information," Brad said. "She just wasn't making sense."

As the hockey season drew to a close in March 1999,
Jane withdrew completely from the Joplins. At the end-
of-season awards banquet, where each of the boys gets a
trophy just for participating that year, Jane and her sons
were absent. Once again, Nancy called Jane repeatedly to
arrange a way for Matt to get his trophy, and to check on
Jane, but she never returned the calls. Months later, Jane
called Nancy out of the blue. She was frantic.

"It's so scary," she told Nancy. "I'm being followed all
of the time now. I have to move, they're hounding me!"

"Jane, let me help you," Nancy said. "Where are you?"

Suddenly, Jane turned on her friend. "They've gotten
to you," she said. "They've turned you against me! Oh no,
they've turned you!"

"What are you talking about?" Nancy implored. "I've
never even met these people!"

Jane started stuttering, stammering, without saying
anything that made sense. Then she hung up. Nancy was
stunned. Jane sounded so terrified that Nancy believed
someone really might be after Jane—though likely not
the powerful Hollywood ghosts she talked about so often.
Nancy tried frantically to get her back on the phone. But

all the numbers Jane had given her over the past year were out of order. With no other contact information, Nancy was powerless to reach out to her.

Like so many other times in her life, Jane simply cut ties with someone close to her, walking away forever. The next time Nancy would hear of Jane, it would be from grisly reports on the nightly news.

10

In the fall of Jason's 1998–1999 school year, the 16-year-old student met with his guidance counselor and made a startling realization—he had enough credits to graduate high school an entire year early, if he wanted to. Jason was a junior, but with the stroke of a pen, he could be considered a senior. He only needed his mother's signature on an authorization slip. To Jason, the knowledge was a chance at freedom. He had grand thoughts of going to college far away—away from Jane. Classmates said Jason always talked a big game, bragging that he was going to attend Harvard Law School someday, maybe becoming a patent attorney. That may have been a bit of a pipe dream, but with a 3.8 GPA, he could have his choice of many a college. Anyway, those who really knew Jason said he was more interested in a computer science career. They got the impression that law school was more his mother's idea.

If Jason expected a fight from his mother over the early graduation request, he would be surprised. She didn't give him one. After all, she herself had graduated a year early from high school. Plus, the earlier he graduated, the earlier he could get a job and help support the family, she reasoned. He would go to college, of course, but he could do that and work part-time, she said. She signed the slip, and Jason became a senior.

There was another reason Jason wanted out of high school early.

"A lot of people thought he was an outcast or a weirdo," a classmate said. Jason had a few friends in school, but not many people considered themselves close to him, mainly because he was never allowed to socialize after school hours, and could never have friends over to his house.

With a hulking 6' 2", 210-pound frame, he could have cut an intimidating figure on campus. But he didn't. He was the butt of many jokes from his meaner classmates, who thought he dressed like a nerd and was kind of a pansy. He was ridiculed behind his back, and sometimes to his face.

Making matters worse, Jason had his own computer, but he wasn't allowed to sign up for an Internet connection at home—Jane was convinced her stalkers could trace her through the Web. For the same reason, the boys weren't allowed cable television, either. So Jason spent countless hours on the computers at school, downloading music and research for classwork, which he took home to watch with Matt. He became very proficient on the keyboard, a talent that left him with a reputation as a geek.

Jason's attitude at school didn't help him make friends, either.

"He always had this belief that he was just better than other people," one former classmate, Joey Gu, said in one newspaper interview. "He thought he was smarter than everyone else, even the teachers."

His high GPA and advanced computer skills turned Jason into a snob. At home, he was nobody. But at school, he was everyone's superior.

As a senior, Jason could sign up to be on the school's

yearbook staff. It gave him a chance to use his computer skills, creating most of the graphics for his own senior class annual.

A fellow yearbook staffer recalled Jason complaining about his mother that year. He hated that she never let him go out. He was 17 years old and wasn't even allowed to date. And a guys' night out was impossible. Sometimes she had a reason for making him stay home, but usually it was just because she wanted him there. He said he wanted to graduate early to get out of the house and far away from her control.

"He would say she was annoying," the friend said. "He complained about her a lot—but what teenager doesn't?"

"I just took what he was saying as being what every teenager says," another friend recalled. "He was just saying, 'I want to get away from my parents and be on my own.' I didn't read anything into it."

But Jason never confided to his friends the real problems at home. Of course, this is a kid who had carefully created a persona for himself in school that revolved around the concept of superiority. He may not have fit in, but it didn't matter. He would excel. That defense mechanism left him with a huge chip on his shoulder, and incapable of confiding a secret like an unstable mother at home. That information would shatter his image as a guy smarter than everyone else. Unlike nearly every other curious high school student experimenting with the freedoms that come with the teenage years—driving, girls, parties, beer—Jason had no freedom. So, instead, he put tough restrictions on himself. He didn't drink, he didn't use drugs, he didn't go to parties. As far as his fellow students were concerned, Jason was a straight-edge, straight-A student bound for big things in life.

But even as graduation loomed, it was clear that Jason was a desperately unhappy young man. Every year, each graduating senior chooses a parting quote to display under his picture. Jason's read:

> I, Jason Bautista, of unsound mind and lacking common sense, wish good will to few people. Instead, I wish bad luck (a lifetime of it) on a lot of people, and laugh at the stupidity of the rest.

Over the summer, 17-year-old Jason got an acceptance letter from California State University at San Bernardino, a thirty-minute drive from home, meaning Jason would continue to live with Jane. Harvard Law School was very far away.

As Jason prepared to start college in the fall, Matt muddled his way through Menifee Middle School. He wasn't the academic star his brother was, instead usually coasting along with B's, C's, and the occasional D. Tall, but with a very thin and wiry build, Matt was much more social than Jason, and liked to goof around with friends in school hallways and chase girls at lunch. He still loved sports, excelling at school baseball games and, most recently, picking up skateboarding—a pal lent Matt a few boards and he became very good. He took to dressing like his fellow skateboarders, too, wearing baggy jeans and T-shirts. He never lost his love for golf, either, and managed to talk Jane into buying him and his big brother their own sets of clubs.

But his favorite game was still hockey.

In the fall of 1999, Matthew had one more chance to develop his skills on the ice. His mom's mental health was so unpredictable, and he hated what she put him through last season. She embarrassed him, often. It was hard to play knowing his mother had had a falling-out with every one of his teammates' parents. But Matt desperately wanted to play. He loved the game and it gave him something to look forward to in a life that was otherwise overwhelmingly unhappy. So, Jane allowed him to sign up again in the fall of 1999, this time with a different set of coaches, managers, and players. It was a clean slate, if only Jane could control herself long enough to let Matt make friends and flourish as a player.

But that was not to be. The 1998 season would be a smashing success compared to what happened the following year.

Again, it was a struggle to get Matt's birth certificate from Jane. She paid all fees in cash, and refused to give out a phone number.

"How will I tell you if a practice is canceled?" a team manager asked her.

"I'll just find out," she said.

During practices, Jane showed up in a large hat pulled low over her face, a long overcoat, huge sunglasses, and gloves. Robert Fowler was the team's manager, and his wife, Francine, was team mom. Their son was on the team. The Fowlers remember Jane's strange appearance and how hard it was to befriend her.

During one practice, Jane approached Francine and tried to explain her odd behavior. "You don't understand," she said. "People are trying to take him away from me."

"Who?" Francine asked.

"My son, Matthew."

"Well, you don't have to worry about that. If there are

people trying to take your son away, there is nobody on this team that would hand him over," Francine assured her.

"You mean to tell me," Jane began, looking intensely at Francine, "that if somebody came up to you right now and offered you forty-five thousand dollars, you would not find a way to give them Matthew?"

"Absolutely not, Jane. Without hesitation, I'd say no. Safety is of the utmost importance. I would never, and nobody on this team would ever, consider something like that. We're a close team and we watch over each other's kids."

Francine remembers Jane visibly relaxing after hearing that. "It seemed to put her at ease. But then I started hearing stories about her burning bridges throughout the team, snapping at everyone. And before I knew it, no one would talk to her."

Jason again came to every practice. He seemed very sad and withdrawn, rarely talking to anyone, and usually passed the time there by losing himself in a book or handheld video game. Francine once told him he shouldn't spend all his time at the rink.

"Don't you have any friends you can go hang out with? You don't have to always be here," Francine told him.

Jason looked over at his mother before looking back at Francine. "No, I don't have any friends."

Jane, however, took the moment to boast about Jason's academic prowess. She told Francine about Jason's early graduation. "It was the only time I ever saw her seem proud of Jason," Francine said. "It was the only time I can really remember her smiling."

Francine was impressed that the quiet, unassuming big kid she saw on the sidelines was actually a brainy guy. Maybe, with any luck, he'd grab a college education and break away from the odd little family headed by his hot-tempered mom.

"Wow, Jason," Francine said, hopeful. "So, what are you going to do now? College?"

"If I let him go," Jane said. "I kind of want him close to home."

Assuming Jane felt that way because she didn't want her young son exposed to frat parties and college drinking a year sooner than he had to be, Francine nodded in agreement. But Jason rolled his eyes.

"I want to go. I really want to go," he said flatly.

Again, Jane refused to let the boys hang out after games. "We had a big van conversion set up with a TV and VCR," Francine related. "All the kids loved to ride in it. But it was never allowed. Even if it was just a ride from a hockey game to a restaurant, they were not allowed to go."

Aside from a team trip to the mountains of Lake Arrowhead, California, where everyone was shocked to see Jane acting jovial and mingling with the kids, she refused all invitations. She declined offers to join the team for meals out or away trips.

Jane also refused to let Matt be a part of the team photograph. "Again, he just wasn't allowed," Francine said. "She said Matthew's father was a very important person in Hollywood with lots of money and he was trying to find Matthew. She said he was a terrible person and if he ever found Matthew, she'd never see her son again."

One frigid November morning, the team had an early game. Francine made up Thermoses of hot chocolate and brought a few dozen doughnuts to help take the sting out of the early morning cold. While chatting with parents as they sat on a bench along the sidelines, Francine noticed Jane standing alone.

"That's not right," she told the other parents.

"Aw, that's just Jane being Jane," one of them responded.

Still, Francine decided to pour Jane a hot cup of cocoa and take it over to her. "Jane, I've got some doughnuts over there, too," she said, extending the cup to Jane as she spoke. "Why don't you come join us?"

Jane stood stoically, refusing to respond.

In that moment, Francine felt deeply sorry for Jane. This woman looked so alone in the world. Francine reached out and put her arm around Jane's shoulders. "Jane, are you okay?" she asked. "Is everything all right?"

Jane turned to look at Francine then, and gave her a look filled with such anger, Francine was startled. "The venom that spewed out of her mouth then!" Francine said. "She attacked my son's skating and accused him of being the favorite boy. She accused me of brown-nosing. I can't even remember all the things she said. But I was so taken aback by all the venom, I just stepped back away from her and, said, 'Wow, okay, if that's how you really feel.' "

"Yeah," Jane spat back. "That's how I really feel."

"Well, that's it then," Francine told her, walking away to rejoin the other parents.

During the next practice, Jane blew up at one of the coaches for making the kids do pushups as part of a punishment for goofing around on the rink. Though everyone had to do them, Jane thought the coach was singling out her son for punishment. "How dare you make my son work that hard! How dare you single him out! And he's got a one hundred and three–degree fever," she screamed.

The coach, Chris Watson, now used to Jane's complaints, answered back, "Well, if he's got a one hundred and three–degree fever, what's he doing here? He has no business being on the ice with a one hundred and three–degree fever!"

That was enough for Coach Watson. He lobbied to have Matthew removed from the team. There was plenty of support for the idea. As much as the coach and others cared about Matthew, his mother made games and practices too difficult for everyone else. Two days later, Robert Fowler had to tell Matt and Jane. He had spent almost three decades working as a deputy sheriff and was used to handling hostile situations. He was ready for Jane if she took the news badly. "I'm well trained in how to deal with mentally ill people, because I deal with so many as a cop," he said. So the duty to break the bad news fell to him.

At the next practice, Fowler pulled Jane aside and explained. "We're removing Matthew from the team. This has nothing to do with your son and has everything to do with you," he told her frankly. "You've become impossible to deal with. And the only reason we've put up with you for so long is because of Matthew. Matthew needs this. But we can't allow you to be here any longer. You'll have to find another club to join. No other team in this league will work with you."

Amazingly, Jane took the news calmly. She grabbed Matt and left the rink. But three days later, at the team's next game, Jane showed up with Matt.

"You don't understand," she told Robert. "If you'd just let me explain . . ."

"I'm sorry, I can't," Robert told her. "You've had too many warnings to change anything now."

"I want him to play," she said.

"Look, Jane, you did this," Robert said. "You did this to your son, nobody else did. This is your fault, with everything you've done to people, the things you've said, your constant arguing and yelling. We can't have that and it has nothing to do with Matthew."

Matthew, standing next to his mother, began to cry. Tears poured down his face as he looked up at Robert, hoping for another chance. Robert was crushed. He knew it wasn't fair that Matthew had to be punished for his mother's behavior. But it was out of his hands. The league wanted her gone. Robert looked down at Matthew and searched for something to say that would ease the blow. He put his arm around him and walked him to the side, out of Jane's hearing.

"Matthew, you did nothing to deserve to be removed from this team," he said as gently as he could. Inside, Robert cringed. If he could have wrapped Matthew up and taken him home with him, he would have. "You're a good athlete. And we loved having you as a part of this team. But it's your mother's behavior. And because of that, I'm very, very sorry. Understand that you are blameless."

"I know" was all Matthew could manage to say.

As Jane left with Matthew, it was Francine's turn to cry. True, she had had a falling-out with Jane just a few days before. But she could sense what a desperate woman Jane was. She turned from Matthew's retreating figure and stared at the team's coaches and managers. "What's going to happen to them?" she asked. "This is all they've got. This team was all that little boy had."

Back at home, chaos erupted. Jane became overwhelmed once again with her paranoia. Why couldn't anyone understand she was under attack? All she was trying to do was protect her small family. People were out to get her, and to get Matthew. She was even becoming suspicious of a male neighbor on the block. Now, it was clear to her, he was a child molester who would stop at nothing to have Matt.

"Even your friends can't be trusted, Matt," Jane told him. "You think those people on that team are on your side? They're all being paid to watch you!"

Jason looked at his mom and shook his head.

"That's crazy," he told her, deciding not to let her ramble on unchallenged tonight. It would have been easier to just let her go, as he had so many, many times in the past. But more often now, his patience ran thin, and he couldn't take it. So tonight, he shouted back. It was one of the few times he ever stood up to Jane.

"There's no one out there after Matt or after you!" he shouted. "You're going fucking nuts!"

Jason was fed up. And maybe, deep down, he was hurt that all of her concern, as misplaced as it may have been, was over herself, and over Matthew. In her fantasy world where bad guys ran amok, not one of them was after Jason. Even in her madness, he was an afterthought.

Jane wasn't going to take that kind of backtalk from Jason. Not now, not tonight, when clearly the rest of the world was out to get her. She couldn't have her oldest son turning on her, too.

"Who got to you?" she countered. "They've paid you off, haven't they? You're on their side!"

"No, nobody 'got to me,' " Jason said, exasperated. "There's nobody out there to pay me off. You're just crazy!"

Frantic with rage, Jane ran into the kitchen and, according to Jason, grabbed a knife. She turned toward her son and waved it at him.

"Who is it?" she demanded. "Who got to you? Who's paying you off?"

A pile of hockey equipment lay spilled on the living room floor near Jason. On instinct, he reached for one of the long sticks and clutched it, jutting the front end in his mother's direction. If she lunged at him with the knife, he would strike her down, hard. But Jane, not the least bit intimidated by her son's determination to fight back, reached down to grab the remaining hockey stick and tossed her knife to the side. They stood there, facing each other, before Jane finally swung the stick at Jason, striking him in the head so hard, a gash split through the skin covering his skull. Blood poured from the wound and Jason threw down his weapon and reached up to touch the cut. As blood stained his fingertips, he began to cry. There was nothing else to do.

That night, Jason ended up in Menifee Valley Medical Center's urgent care unit, where a doctor stapled up the gash. Jane warned the boy before he stepped foot inside the emergency room to keep quiet about their scuffle.

"You'll be really sorry if you start any trouble in there," she told him.

The doctor had little reason to be alarmed by the cut. Just another teenage boy who thought he was invincible. Boys playing too hard and ending up with a gash or a broken bone were normal fare in his business. But to make conversation, the doctor asked, "So, what happened to you tonight?"

It would have been an easy moment for Jason to tell someone, maybe triggering at long last an investigation by social workers into his deeply unhappy, deeply troubled home life. But he said nothing. Instead, he told exactly the kind of story the doctor expected to hear—Jason had been goofing around with his little brother, playing sword games with their hockey sticks, and he accidentally got whacked.

It took seven staples to close the gash, and the blow left a permanent three-inch scar. But it didn't matter. Jason silently took the pummeling, then lied to his doctor, successfully protecting his mentally ill mother from exposure.

11

Since the time she'd bolted from her mother's home in Winthrop Harbor, Jane had tried to distance herself from her parents. She still hated them. But she exchanged letters regularly with her grandmother and sent her grandparents gifts during birthdays and Christmas, even talked on the phone with her mother and father from time to time. In 1997, she went home for a summer weekend visit. Despite the minimal contact, her family still saw the change in Jane. Clearly, she was paranoid about something, but, for the most part, she seemed rational. So her family just ignored her oddities. Jane had always been a quirky and temperamental woman in need of constant attention. Her flair for drama had obviously become more pronounced now that she was older.

But two years later, Jane's condition was considerably worse. She agreed, for her grandparents' sake, to see them for Christmas. She and the boys stayed at her grandparents' house the first few days of the visit.

Her parents came next door to visit with their estranged daughter and grandsons, hoping to repair the broken relationship. But, as expected, Jane immediately clashed with her mom and dad. She told them that she was being stalked by powerful people—who wanted to do her harm. Her babbling made little sense. And Nellie knew her daughter was, at this point in life, deeply disturbed.

They tried to tell Jane she wasn't thinking straight, an accusation that sent her into a rage. By day four of the family reunion, Jane made a tearful call to an old family friend, Cathy Atchinson, asking to stay at her place for the rest of the visit. Her mother was coming over too much and she couldn't take it anymore, she told Cathy. She needed out. And she needed a ride. Her grandfather, Ben Funderburk, was desperate to keep her at home, she said. So desperate, he'd snuck out one evening and let all the air out of the tires on her rental car.

It's not clear why Jane's family didn't try to get her psychiatric help then. There was no longer any doubt—Jane was mentally ill and her family knew it.

After her daughter's murder, Nellie would testify in court about Jane's mental stability. Asked if she knew in 1999 that her daughter's condition had worsened, Nellie answered, "Truthfully, yes," and broke into tears.

Yet during that visit, when Jane's disturbed mind was veering out of control, instead of getting her help, instead of trying to get her committed, or at least evaluated by a doctor, they told her she wasn't making sense, then watched her walk out the door.

It's a particularly sad footnote in the life story of Jane Bautista when you take into consideration that her family was well off financially and could have easily afforded the best of medical care for her. Instead, they chose to offer her support in the form of monthly certified checks. When asked if she'd thought about the welfare of her grandsons, Nellie testified, "They were worries, yes." Still, the family did nothing.

Cathy was unaware of how troubling Jane's inner demons had become. She visited Jane at her San Marcos home in 1991, during a vacation in California, and they talked periodically by phone. Cathy hadn't been close to Jane in years. Still, she considered her a friend. So when she called begging for help, Cathy gladly picked up her old pal and took her to her mother's house in Salem, where Cathy was spending the holidays. Cathy's mother, Bonnie Salyards, had known the Osbornes since 1966, when she and her husband moved to Zion for a few years and lived next door to them. Jane was just 4 years old. Bonnie remembered a bright, outgoing, fun-loving little girl who frequently asked to play with little Cathy. Now, looking at 38-year-old Jane Bautista, Bonnie was shocked. Jane had let her appearance go, and her ramblings started almost immediately.

"My house," she began shortly after putting down her bags. "It's bugged. You wouldn't believe it. But it's true. And it's someone very rich and famous who's doing it all. I can't tell you who it is, but If I told you his name, you'd recognize it."

She went on for a very long time with her tales, Bonnie remembered. She told Bonnie, "I can't even leave my house anymore except at night. It makes it harder for them to see me if I leave at night."

It wasn't the first time Bonnie and her daughter had heard wild tales from Jane. During Jane's 1997 visit, Cathy's family had spent the day with Jane and her boys. Jane was in good spirits and the two women talked eagerly as they caught up on each other's lives. But abruptly, Jane changed. Cathy tried to tell Jane about her sister's new boyfriend, a roadie for the band Rage Against the Machine. Jane's mood blackened. "Oh no, they're no good!" Jane said. "They can't be trusted, you have to tell her that! No one from the music industry can be trusted!"

Cathy thought the comments were strange, but didn't think it meant her friend had gone crazy. It wasn't until her visit during Christmas of 1999 that it became clear—Jane Bautista was mentally ill.

Jane stayed one night. The next morning, she rented a car, packed up her sons, and drove away for good. She talked about going to Michigan for a while, though as far as anyone can tell, she simply went back to California. That 1999 trip was the last time Jane would ever visit home again. And it was the last time her family or childhood friends would see her alive.

Back at home, Jason was settling into college life very well at California State University–San Bernardino. He wasn't sure yet what he wanted to do with his life, but he was leaning toward something in the sciences.

He paid for school through financial aid, which he easily qualified for, since his mother hadn't held a job of any kind since he was a boy. With no discernable source of income for the family to report, aside from Jason's monthly Social Security checks stemming from his father's death, Jason was entitled to a state grant to cover tuition fees, and low-interest school loans to cover books and living expenses. It could have been a time of amazing independence for him. He even held down his first part-time job, working as a clerk for a mail order company, Starcrest Products, located in the nearby city of Perris. Mostly, he answered phones and took care of the mail, but he loved the extra time away from home. Yet at 17 years old, he was still a minor. So, despite his graduation from high school and his college enrollment, he was still bound to his mother's home.

In the spring of 2000, Jane's behavior once again seemed to stabilize. She still had no real friends to speak of. But there may have been times in her life when she longed for them.

Jane hadn't spoken to her old friend and San Marcos neighbor Paula Beam Toedt since 1996, and they hadn't really been close friends since the disastrous skiing trip in Big Bear that January. So it was a shock when Paula, arms heavy with groceries as she bounded up the steps to her home, saw Jane standing outside.

"Jane, what are you doing here?" a startled Paula said.

"I can't use the phone anymore," she said. "My telephone is bugged, so if I need to talk to anybody, I just have to go to their house."

It was a typically cryptic Jane statement, so Paula rolled her eyes and let her former neighbor inside. She moved into the kitchen to unpack groceries, and Jane followed. Jane chatted about nothing particularly eventful at first, just catching her up on Jason's graduation and college plans. Then she started.

"I have to talk to someone, but my house is bugged," she said. Then, lowering her voice, she added, "I wouldn't be surprised if your house was bugged, too. You better be careful."

Paula just laughed uncomfortably at Jane. "She was just out of her mind, it was obvious," Paula said.

"Well, I'm just trying to warn you. Someone is out to get me, you know," she told Paula.

The visit was brief, but before she left, she turned to Paula, now carefully putting away her empty grocery bags.

"So, you really do this stuff, huh?"

"Do what, Jane?"

"You buy groceries and you cook?"

"Of course I do. Don't you?" Paula asked.

"Oh never," Jane told her, shaking her head. "I'd never do something like that."

As she left, Paula called her husband. "Maybe it's one of her new Arab boyfriends out to get her," he joked, remembering Jane's old habit of dating foreign men.

"No, I think she's just finally lost whatever was left of her mind," Paula answered.

12

Until now, life with Jane had been hard. She was unpredictable, temperamental, verbally abusive, and sometimes physically abusive. She kept her sons on edge with her stories of imaginary people out to get her, out to get Matt.

But all of that would be a cakewalk compared to the life they were about to endure.

In the summer of 2000, Jane's insanity took another turn for the worse. A pattern began to set in, with Jane quieting down in the late spring to early summer. She was never normal, but she was calmer. Then, as fall approached, and particularly as the winter holidays neared, she seemed to lose her grip again. And each time her sickness flared, it grew more intense.

Even though years had passed, Jane still hung on to her belief that Duncan Sheik was out to get her. The idea reemerged so strongly that summer, she decided to call the police. An officer came to the door, and Jane tried to explain that her life was in danger.

"The man on this CD, this singer, he's out to kill me," she said. "I met him a long time ago and told him about my life. Then he used the things I said in his songs and now he wants me gone!"

The officer knew a 51/50 (the police radio code for a mentally ill person) when he saw one. He patiently listened to her rantings for a few minutes, then took the

CD she shoved into his hand before he turned to leave. It was obvious the officer didn't believe her tale, and Jane, even in her deluded state, could tell.

"You see that?" she told her boys. "Now even the police are against us!"

Days later, Jason and Matt discovered their mother in her room frantically packing.

"We have to get out of here," she told them, her voice filled with fear. "They're watching us, right now. The whole house is covered with cameras."

She was in such a state of panic, neither boy knew what to do. So they helped her pack. She rented a moving van and loaded it up with every piece of furniture in the house. Neither boy knew where, exactly, they were headed. But Jane didn't seem in the mood to answer questions. The goal was to get out of the Menifee house immediately. She'd figure out what to do next when they were on the road.

Jane never spoke to her neighbors as she pulled out. Dan Cormier never even got a chance to say goodbye to his athletic protégé. She simply left, on the run from the latest set of enemies living in her head.

Before deciding where to settle down, Jane made a stop at Sun City Mini Storage, just a short drive from the Menifee house. She dumped most of the furniture there, then spent several weeks at a Best Western hotel in Beaumont, California. Jason lost his job at Starcrest over the abrupt move. Ever the survivor, he applied for a clerking job at the hotel and got it. However, he'd only be there two months before Jane decided it was time to move again. She spent considerable time scouting out towns before finding one that just might be safe.

This time, Jane made her way to the tiny town of Wildomar, California, with an average population of just over

14,000. It was just about ten miles south of Menifee, but Jane decided it was secure. For now. Just in case, she kept most of the family's belongings in storage. She wanted to be free to run on a moment's notice, if necessary.

Oddly, she did take on an obligation that seemed out of character for a woman on the run. One day, she decided she wanted a pet. So Matt and Jason drove to the local pound and picked up a puppy. The dog would become the one object in her life that Jane would shower with love and attention. She took the dog everywhere with her, and treated it like a member of the family. For that, Jason hated the puppy. It's obvious what must have been running through his mind as he watched his mom, the one who could be so hateful, so angry with him all of the time, lavish time, love, and attention on a pet. How could she be so kind and loving to a mutt from the pound, and yet so cold and cruel to her own child?

On August 25, 2000, Jason turned 18 years old. Technically, there was nothing stopping him now from packing his bags and leaving Jane's life for good. But he didn't. Only three months after leaving the Best Western, he started working at the front desk at the Country Inn in Corona, bringing in a few hundred dollars extra a month. Though at 18 he no longer got the monthly Social Security benefits from his father's death, he was doing well, and certainly could have made it financially on his own— or at least with the help of a roommate. Unlike most areas of California, where the rent on even the smallest one-bedrooms can run $1,000 a month or more, apartments around California State University–San Bernardino ran about $800 monthly for a two-bedroom.

But Jason didn't pick up even one of the countless

flyers littering the school campus, all in search of a room-mate. Instead, he remained home. If only he'd known what a profound mistake he was making.

Shortly after Jason turned 18, the family bought a second car. It was a big deal for Jason—with his own car came added freedom. It was a matter of practicality, really, that prompted Jane's generosity. With Jason's part-time work and full-time school schedule, sharing a car was too im-practical. So Jane relented and bought a brand-new 2000 gray Oldsmobile Intrigue. Well, actually, Jane and Jason bought the car together. Since Jane had no job and no work history, she couldn't qualify for a car loan without a co-signer. That came from her son, who at least was em-ployed and had student loan income. The new car was a giant step up from the family's old car, a late eighties model blue Honda Accord that had definitely seen better days. One of the back windows was even missing, mak-ing it hard to use for travel on rainy days.

Jason thought that, as a co-signer on the car, and with his school and work money helping to pay bills, he would get to share the shiny new car with his mother.

"No way," she told him. "You take the Accord. That's your car now."

The news infuriated him. He resented having to drive the ugly car all the time, especially since his money was going to a share of the payments on the Intrigue. But with little choice, he picked up the Honda's keys and shoved them in his pocket.

13

Living in Wildomar didn't satisfy Jane for long. Jason saw the signs coming. Only four months passed before, once again, some neighbor—the man just across the street—had become part of the conspiracy against her. He watched their house, watched her come and go, she said.

"He must be on their payroll," she told her boys. "I can't believe it. They're getting to everyone! We've got to get out of here."

She also believed her life was now being taped and broadcast on Mexican television stations. "I know, because all the Mexicans know me. They always look at me and laugh," she said.

It was time to pack up and run. This time at night, so the neighbor couldn't see them. With fewer belongings, they packed in a matter of minutes. She stuffed everything she could into the family cars, and left behind anything that wouldn't fit. Then she drove furiously, a few miles into the city of Hemet, where she booked the family into another hotel. Of course, her beloved dog came along, too. In the morning, she would find a temporary kennel for it.

After that close call, she would take no more chances lugging belongings. Even though most of the family's furniture was in the Sun City storage unit, she still had mattresses, Jason's computer, and the family TV to worry about—much too much to move when you're running for your life. So she opened a second unit at West Florida Self Storage in Hemet and dumped everything but an armload of clothes for each of them, stored in the car trunk.

Life for the boys got dramatically worse after leaving Wildomar. For more than a year, Jane refused to find another place to live. Instead, the family checked in and out of motels all over eastern California. She never stayed in one place too long, certainly never more than a week or so. That would give the bad guys time to find her, Jane reasoned. So, the family constantly moved.

Worst of all for the boys were the nights when Jane skipped renting a room altogether and forced her family to sleep in their cars—Jane and Matt in the Oldsmobile, Jason in his Honda.

Periodically, Jane picked up her beloved dog from the Moreno Valley kennel where she kept him most of the time, and he slept in the car, too. But what the boys hated most of all was the lack of everyday amenities—they couldn't shower, they had no bathroom, they had no television. They were homeless, and it was humiliating.

Jason begged Jane to get another apartment. He despised living this way—getting ready for work and school from the trunk of his car, searching for a bathroom where he could brush his teeth and wash up. It's why he liked working as a desk clerk at the hotels. It gave him access to showers and washrooms. But that wasn't good enough. Jason wanted to go home each night after school, like every other kid his age.

Jason would later call this time the worst of his life. "It was so horrible," he said after his mother's death. "We were homeless for a year and a half. I couldn't even sign any leases because she didn't trust anyone. Everybody was always out to get us. It was horrible. My life was so miserable. I wanted to kill myself. I contemplated suicide so many times, you don't even know."

Faced with the prospect of sleeping in a car each night, the boys could only look forward to the times when they had a hotel room for a night or two. At least then they'd have a hot shower, cable, maybe even access to a swimming pool and hot tub. But at times, Jane chose motels that were simply dirty, and attracted the worst of society. Prostitutes, drug addicts, and the mentally ill often hung in the halls of such places, some with vouchers from the state to cover rooming expenses, because they had recently been released from institutions and had nowhere else to go. Some nights, the smells and noise would be so bad, a decent night's sleep was impossible.

Their wandering became so erratic, Matthew simply could not attend high school five days a week. By this time, Jane was too concerned over his safety to let him go to classes anyway. Just because they were on the run, however, didn't mean Matt would grow up uneducated, she decided.

That was the funny thing about Jane—through all of her madness, she was not a stupid woman. She still showed signs of being an educated lady from a well-to-do family. She was articulate and could still reason well, as long as the topic had nothing to do with the big conspiracy. Ultimately, Jane decided no one could teach her son better than she could. So, in the winter of 2000, she enrolled Matthew in a home-school program through the Redlands Unified School District, a small area in San Bernardino County. Under the program, Matt checked in with a supervising teacher every several weeks. The teacher issued him his books, lesson plans, and tests, and gave out his final grades. But Jane oversaw his day-to-day classwork. It was the perfect situation for Jane, leaving her son without restrictions to roam at his mother's bidding.

Meanwhile, Jason's grade point average fell so dramatically, the university put him on academic probation, meaning he'd have to pull up his grades by the next quarter or he'd end up suspended. But as life on the run continued, Jason couldn't get his grades together, and he was barred from campus. It's not clear if Jason told Jane about the expulsion, but he didn't need her rantings to feel devastated by the blow. For a kid who'd always seen himself as an academic achiever, the expulsion cut deep into his self-esteem. He took solace by blaming his crazy home life. And he was determined not to let it interrupt his education. Jason enrolled at San Jacinto Community College in Menifee, attending for a semester until he pulled his grades up enough to re-enroll at the San Bernardino college.

Each day, as Jason went on his way to work or school, Jane would have to decide if she'd be in a motel or not by the time he returned. If not, she would give him a meeting place to find her, usually the parking lot of a fast food restaurant. Because Jane didn't allow cell phones, Jason couldn't call her and find out where they'd be. He'd simply have to cruise the designated parking lot in search of her car. It was hard for Jason to tell exactly what Jane did with his little brother, and sometimes the family dog, all day long—especially during those times when they had no room. Likely, they simply drove around for hours. Sometimes, when Jane was having a good day, they'd go to the movies or maybe even a ballgame. Sometimes they'd walk the malls or settle into a library so Matthew could do some homework. It was a crazy, fly-by-the-seat-of-your-pants kind of life, with no end in sight.

As his family hopped from motel to motel, Jason continued taking on front desk jobs. After working for Best Western in Beaumont for two months, then clerking at the Country Inn in Corona for fourteen months, he landed a job at the Holiday Inn in Ontario by February 2001.

Holiday Inn General Manager Dan Huffer was impressed with Jason right away. As Dan remembers, Jason was "respectable, polite, always stood up straight, and said, 'Yes sir,' 'No sir' so much, you'd think he had a military upbringing." His goodie-two-shoes manner easily won him the respect of his boss. "If you wanted a really good person on the front desk, he was your guy."

Over time, Jason regularly won "employee of the month" awards, some even at the encouragement of customers impressed by his helpful and overwhelmingly friendly attitude.

But interestingly, co-workers at the Holiday Inn remember a very different side of Jason. While he was always respectful to superiors, he was rude to his equals. True, he had a reputation for being a smart guy and a capable employee. But personally, he was a "smart-aleck," according to one employee, and hard to get along with. Certainly, the stress of a vagabond life was enough to push anyone into a perpetual bad mood. Likely, he was so unhappy at home, it was hard to switch gears and remain cheerful at work. But it was frustrating for co-workers to see him so cheerful to bosses, and so unpleasant to them. Plus, he rarely talked about his home life. He never told a soul about his year of homelessness and living in motels.

He was too proud for that. So co-workers had no idea.
They just thought Jason was, best case scenario, weird;
worst case, an ass.

"He always thought he knew more than other people,"
one co-worker said. "And a lot of times, he did. I have to
give it to him, he was a smart guy. He always liked to use
big words and was real formal, even to his co-workers.
But most people just thought he was kind of weird."

Casey Kritzer, a bartender at the hotel, was one of the
few to develop a friendship with Jason. She was married,
so there never was a chance for anything but friendship
between him and the young woman. But they were close
enough that they often hung out together after work. It
was one of the few friendships Jason had had over his
lifetime.

Despite his kindness toward Casey, Jason was so abrupt
and patronizing toward other co-workers, he quickly
earned a reputation as being difficult to work with. He
was bossy and critical, convinced no one could do the
front desk job better than he could, including his managers. One female employee said she thought Jason was
particularly condescending to the females on the job. She
may have been right. It's possible that Jason, unable to
lash out at Jane, badgered his female co-workers instead.
At any rate, her run-ins with him became so frequent,
she complained to front office manager Priscilla Ramos
and hotel manager Crystal Cantu, telling them, "Either
he goes, or I do." Instead, Crystal, a very no-nonsense
businesswoman who had run the hotel for seven years,
warned Jason about his behavior and put him on probation. She was suspicious of his two-faced behavior and
told him so.

The warning put Jason in check. Though behind his

back, co-workers still considered him a jerk, at least he tempered his outbursts enough to keep his job.

Months later, Jason started training as the night auditor for the hotel. He still worked the desk, but the added responsibility meant he'd earn an extra $2 an hour. "To my mind, Jason was one of the best employees we had," Dan said. "He always did a good job."

With no home to return to at the end of his work and school day, Jason tried to stay as busy as possible. So when a classmate invited him to join the school's Chemistry Club, he jumped at the chance. "Plus," his friend told him, "there's free pizza at every meeting!"

Jason didn't need the pizza enticement. He loved the group.

"Jason was one of the few people who came to almost every meeting and every event we had that year," said Stacie Eldridge, club president during the 2001–2002 school year. "He was very active that year."

A chief goal for the club was promoting science, specifically chemistry, among kids, hoping to plant enough interest that they'd one day choose the major, too. Jason loved the events with kids. For Halloween, the university held a fall festival, complete with game booths and rides, open to the community. The Chemistry Club set up a booth that would teach kids how to make green slime. Jason volunteered to work the booth while wearing a Scooby-Doo costume.

"Come over, kids, come on by," Jason shouted from beneath the giant Scooby-Doo head. "Learn how to make slime!" And Jason slipped a handful of candy to every kid that came by.

"He was always throwing in humor for the kids and

trying to make things fun for them," Stacie said. "He wanted to show them that science doesn't have to be serious all the time. Like, 'Look, we're having a great time and we're doing science! It doesn't have to be scary.'"

It was the same thing a month later when Stacie organized a promotional event at the San Bernardino County Museum. Kids could come by and learn how to conduct a series of chemistry experiments. "And Jason loved it," Stacie said. "He was the biggest kid of all, laughing with them and really getting into showing them what to do. He loved to help people. That's the Jason I knew."

In the beginning, his Chem Club pals considered Jason standoffish.

"His life wasn't an open book," Stacie said. "He didn't just tell you things about himself. It took a while to get to know him."

But after seeing him with the kids, he won the Chem Club's respect and friendship. A small group of them often hung out in a lunchroom on campus, drinking coffee, reading the paper, talking sports. Jason became one of the regulars. He was there almost every lunch, usually poring over the sports pages he loved so much. Friends thought he was a little bit obsessed with his favorite games—basketball and football. During football season, he made bets with as many of the Chemistry Club guys as would take him on. And during March Madness, when college basketball teams sweat it out for a chance at the championship title, nobody knew each university's statistics and shots for winning better than Jason.

"He could be a little high-strung when it came to talking about sports," Stacie said. "He could get all riled up about it. But mostly, he was a fun guy. He had friends in the club, lots of friends. If anything, when Jason was around, he just added to the good time."

It's an amazing admission, given all that was going on in Jason's personal life. He could have been a miserable, bitter young man by this time. But somehow, someway, Jason pushed aside the bitterness created by living in a car and out of motels, and he simply made the most of college life. The gap between his life with Jane and his life with the rest of the world grew wider. And suddenly, he understood what it could be like to live free from the constraints of a mentally ill mother.

14

Jane refused to even look at an apartment for the entire year of 2001. Increasingly, the family slept in the car. But on the heels of 2002, as the winter nights got colder and Christmas quickly approached, Jane rented her family a low-end motel room in the city of Corona. It was so dirty, Jason thought about sleeping in his car anyway. But it was the only place Jane considered "safe for the night."

Jason had had enough. He was miserable. And his grades, the one thing he always took pride in, plummeted from A's to C's. Matt wasn't happy either, but where could he go? What could he do? Only Jason was old enough to walk away if he wanted. And finally, he decided to do just that.

"You know what?" he told her. "I think I'm going to go ahead and move out. You guys can always get your own one-bedroom apartment if you want. We could probably find two one-bedroom apartments for the same rate as one two-bedroom. But I just have to get stable. I have to get my stuff done, my schoolwork, and I can't the way we are now."

"You're bluffing," Jane responded, refusing to believe her son would actually walk out on her. "You don't have what it takes to live on your own."

But the next morning, he packed up his belongings from the hotel room and drove away. And when he left, it was in the Intrigue, the car his mother always drove. Still asleep inside the hotel room, it would be hours before she would realize her car was gone.

In truth, this was no spur-of-the-moment decision. Jason had been considering the move for a long time. He just needed to muster up the courage to make it happen. Then he learned that a former high school classmate taking classes at California State University–Pomona was getting his own apartment. It meant he'd be leaving his dorm room a month early, and he offered to let Jason crash there. That would give Jason time to get some cash together to rent his own place. Jason was only a few weeks away from getting another student loan check to cover the spring quarter—more than enough to put a down payment on a place.

But the next night, Jane tossed a wrench into her son's plans for independence.

Jason was working a shift at the hotel that evening when his mother showed up at the front desk. Bracing for the embarrassing confrontation to come, he quickly escorted her outside and into the front parking lot.

Dan remembered the incident clearly. He didn't hear the argument, but it was obvious from Jane's mannerisms that she was not happy. "You could see her lighting into him, just screaming and yelling," Dan said. "And he just stood there and took it . . . All I could figure was, this was a young man who led two lives—work and school were his escape from his home life."

Outside, a deeply embarrassed Jason simply hung his head.

"You're not going to do this to me," she began. "Your father ran out on me and I'm not going to stand for it from you, too."

As her voice grew louder, Jason tried to keep her calm. "Mom, I'm not running out. It's just time I tried to make it on my own," he explained.

But Jane would not be reasoned with. Instead, she looked at him, her eyes wild, her voice low, but forceful. "I made a promise to myself. I promised nobody would ever run out on me again. I won't let that happen. You won't treat me like your father did!"

It had been a long time since Jane had compared Jason to his father. He had committed suicide when Jason was just a toddler, but in Jane's mind, the hurt from that tragedy was as fresh as if it had happened yesterday.

Jason looked at his mother, wild with anger, and said nothing. He knew from past experience that the more said, the more crazed she could become. But she said nothing else. Instead, she turned and walked toward the Intrigue, pulled out a set of keys, and drove it away. Jason had forgotten that there was a spare set. And now she was using it to drive the car home, leaving Jason stranded. He had known better than to take the Intrigue instead of the Accord. He was already provoking her wrath by moving out; to take the car she considered to be hers on top of everything else was asking for way too much.

Shaken, but undeterred in his decision, Jason slowly made his way back inside the hotel lobby. "Looks like I'm moving, so I'll need a change of address form as soon as possible," he said.

But in truth, Jason had no idea what he was going to do. He had no car. How would he make it to school when morning broke in just a few hours? Or to his friend's dorm to change clothes, take a shower, and get some sleep, before returning for his graveyard shift that night?

By morning, Jason had managed to talk a co-worker

into giving him a ride to school when their shift ended, and later, a classmate offered to give him a ride home after class. But, afraid he wouldn't find a ride to work, he had his pal drop him off in Ontario, even though it was 3 in the afternoon and his shift didn't start until 11 p.m. To kill time, he walked to a nearby mall and just sat, trying to figure out a plan. He couldn't think. Exhausted, he considered calling Jane.

"I hadn't taken a shower in two days," Jason would later say about that afternoon in the mall. "I was dirty. I was tired. I was cold. So I gave in. I called her at that motel she was at in Corona."

Jason wasn't even sure if she'd still be there, but he decided that if she was, he'd give up trying to live on his own. After a few rings, Jane picked up the phone.

"Come pick me up," he said simply.

Jane and Matt met Jason at the mall and then drove to Pomona to pick up his clothes. Along the way, Jane taunted her son about his failed stab at independence.

"I knew this would happen," she said. "I knew you'd have to come back, because you don't have a choice. You have nowhere else to go."

Jason sat quietly listening to his mother gloat. But in his head, he thought, "I'll be okay. I'll be okay. I just want to go home, take a shower, and do whatever it takes to get through this life."

That's when Jason thought about it. Killing her.

It's hard to know if he'd ever entertained the idea before. But if he had, he'd never talked about it. Now, as he sat in his beat-up Honda Accord with his little brother, he whispered the idea to Matt. "I wish she was dead," he began.

Matt didn't respond. He knew his brother hated his mom. Hell, they both hated her. But to wish her dead?

"Wouldn't it be great if we got rid of Mom?" he said. "I'm just saying, you know, life would be a hell of a lot easier without her around."

"Yeah, I know it would," Matt chuckled, hoping to lighten the conversation. "I mean, it wouldn't be great if she got killed or something, but yeah, it would be great if she was gone." Then he looked away and said nothing else on the subject. Jason was just mad and blowing off steam, Matt reasoned. He'd never really hurt her. He was too much of a wuss. He couldn't even stand up to her when she yelled at him, or that time when she'd knocked him in the head with a hockey stick. No, he wouldn't hurt her. He didn't have the guts.

Fortunately, life stabilized after Jason's failed attempt to leave home. Jane regained some of her grip on sanity, even allowing the family to stay in a Corona motel for several weeks. Jason used the time to try to reason once again with Jane.

"Please," he begged. "You've got to try and get us an apartment. My grades are so bad. I need to be stable. And so does Matthew. He needs to be in school and around kids his own age, can't you see that?"

"I can't," she told him. "I just don't think I can do it."

"Yes, you can," he persisted. "Just try. While I'm at school today, you and Matthew go look for a place to rent, okay?"

His financial aid check had finally come in, so the family now had the extra cash needed to cover a security deposit and a month's rent. Now was the time to act, Jason told her. Jane was hesitant, but she relented. She was still

scared, but even Jane was tired of running. She promised
Jason she'd look.

It was never easy finding a place to live. Jane had no
proof of income, because she had no job. Grandma Mae's
monthly check stubs were not enough for most landlords.
Add to that Jane's hyper-sense of distrust for almost
everyone, and finding an apartment would be a huge un-
dertaking.

But Jane actually thought she'd found a place she liked
in the well-groomed, upper-middle-class town of Redlands, California. It felt safe, and, in truth, she had stumbled onto one of the safest cities in the county. While
neighboring San Bernardino had to contend with rampant
teenage pregnancies, poverty, meth labs, and a dozen or
more murders a year, Redlands had no such problems.
Year after year could pass with not a single homicide case
to keep detectives busy.

Somehow, despite Jane's sketchy background, the land-
lord at a well-kept apartment complex approved the family's application on a two-bedroom place. But the approval
immediately sent Jane backpedaling.

"I don't trust it," she said. "The manager over there is
against us. We can't take it."

She applied to a complex in another well-to-do community in Rancho Cucamonga, located in San Bernardino
County. This time, Jane's flimsy income status wasn't
good enough and the application was rejected. Of course,
Jane interpreted that to mean the obvious. She went on a
rampage.

"You see! They hate us! It's because they're Jews and
all the Jews have turned against us," she said.

The boys thought they'd never have a home again. For
weeks, Jane gave up the hunt entirely. They went back to

motel living. But Jason wasn't ready to give up. After patiently giving his mother time to cool down, he broached the subject again, this time taking a new approach.

He still hated arguing with his mother, but he had become an expert at playing off her compulsions. Education was one of them. Matt was another.

"I heard there's a new high school opening in Riverside," he mentioned as casually as he could. "What do you think? That might be a good place to look. Maybe Matt would like going to a brand-new school." Then he threw in the words he knew would best play on his mom's obsession with academics. "A new school means new books, new supplies, new everything. That could be a chance for him to get a really good education."

Remarkably, she took Jason's advice and resumed the hunt for a home, this time in Riverside, near the new school. It was a blistering hot summer day as Jane cruised up and down the city streets in search of a place to live. Summers in Riverside could be brutal, routinely busting the 100-degree mark. But it was one of the characteristics that made the area so affordable to live in. Riverside and San Bernardino Counties made up a dry, hot, unattractive region of California known as "the Inland Empire" because of its remote location from the beaches that make sunny Southern California such a popular place to live and play. Late summers in Riverside were the worst. With any luck, they'd find a place—preferably with air-conditioning—before June disappeared.

It wasn't long before Jane drove by a large cluster of apartments just on the outskirts of town, bordering nearby Moreno Valley. It was a bland complex, no different from any of a thousand that might be found in any place across America—just a series of huge, white stucco buildings

surrounded by a maze of parking spaces. For some reason
understood only by the muddled mind of Jane Bautista, this
place on Alessandro Boulevard would finally be home.
Once again, Jane's application by herself was not enough
to be approved. But Jason, a full-time student with proof
of financial aid and regular paychecks from his part-time
job, could co-sign the lease. It was enough to win approval. The boys held their breath waiting for their mom's
reaction. Would she now decide, as she had in the past,
that this place was ultimately no good? But she didn't.
She held her tongue and said nothing.

Finally, after a year and a half of life on the road, in
hotels, sleeping in cars, the vagabond life was over. They
had an apartment. And the boys were overjoyed.

It was a good time for the Bautista family. Jane agreed
that Matt could return to regular classes. By late July,
she'd enrolled him in Martin Luther King High School.
Come August, when the school year began, Matthew
would be a sophomore at the new campus. Matt, never the
best student, actually looked forward to going back to
regular school, where he could be around peers again,
and make friends.

For now, life had returned to normal. The boys knew it
might not last long. But they couldn't think about that now.
Instead, they dove into the routines of adolescent life and
just hoped their mother held the monsters in her mind at
bay for as long as possible.

15

With home life stabilized, Jason took on more responsibility at school. He entered his junior year at California State University–San Bernardino, and officially declared biochemistry as his major. He loaded up on chemistry classes and continued volunteering with the Chemistry Club.

But the most significant change for Jason that year was his new on-campus job, which he took that September, while still maintaining his graveyard shifts at the Ontario Holiday Inn.

The school offered a computer lab set aside for the university's School of Chemistry and Biology students. Always the computer geek, Jason spent a lot of time there anyway. Jane's delusions of being broadcast on various websites meant she forbade her son to connect to the Internet from home. At the lab, he could surf the Net for hours if he wanted to.

"He wasn't exactly a brilliant computer student, but he was better than average," said California State University Professor Ken Mantei, who helped oversee the computer lab. So Jason was hired, earning $6.70 an hour. With his new job came keys to the lab, where he could come and go as he pleased at all hours of the day and night, according to Mantei. Occasionally he brought along Matt, who sometimes did homework, but mostly played video games

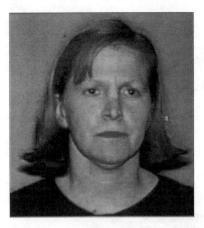

Jane Bautista in her December 2000 driver's license photo. Jane's paranoia prevented her from appearing in many photos, so the photo from the Department of Motor Vehicles was the only picture investigators had of the victim.
(*Courtesy Orange County Sheriff's Department*)

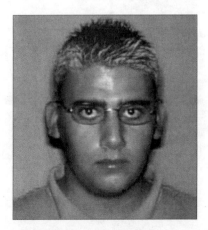

Jason Bautista in his July 1999 driver's license photo.
Jane also disliked her boys' appearing in photos.
(*Department of Motor Vehicles photo*)

Pete Martinez, the security guard who broke the case open for police when he stumbled on the boys as they tried to dump Jane's body. He's pictured in front of his Oceanside guard shack, which sat just a few feet away from the Dumpster Jason and Matthew wanted to use to dispose of their mother's body.
(*Photo by Eliza Gano*)

Doorway into the Riverside apartment where Jane last lived with her sons.
(*Courtesy Orange County Sheriff's Department*)

Booking mug shot of Matthew Montejo.
(*Courtesy Orange County Sheriff's Department*)

Booking mug shot of Jason Bautista.
(*Courtesy Orange County Sheriff's Department*)

Senior Deputy District Attorney Michael Murray.
(*Photo by Tina Dirmann*)

Matthew Montejo's room at the Riverside apartment. It was the room he shared with Jason before Jane's death. After her murder, the boys replaced the sleeping bags they used to sleep in with mattresses.
(*Courtesy Orange County Sheriff's Department*)

The site off Ortega Highway where Jason dumped his mother.
(*Courtesy Orange County Sheriff's Department*)

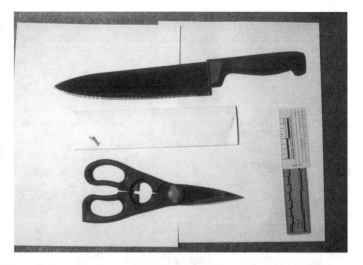

The kitchen knife Jason used to cut off his mom's head and hands. He used the scissors to chop off her hair, making her neck more visible before he began slicing.
(*Courtesy Orange County Sheriff's Department*)

Homicide investigator Craig Johnson at his desk within the offices of the Orange County Sheriff Department's Homicide Unit.
(*Photo by Tina Dirmann*)

Investigator Andre Spencer reviews one of the dozen thick case files
collected in the Bautista homicide.
(Photo by Tina Dirmann)

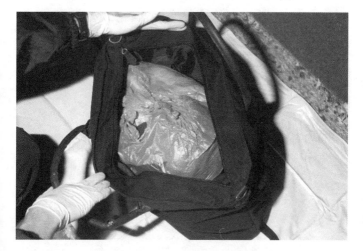

Investigators discover the bag carrying Jane's head and hands in her Riverside
apartment. The remains were double wrapped inside grocery bags before they
were stuffed into the carrying case.
(Courtesy Orange County Sheriff's Department)

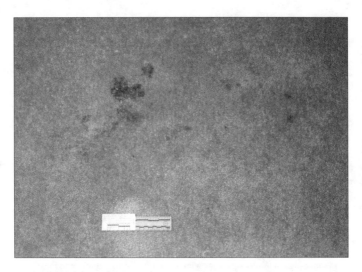

A few splashes of blood stained the living room carpet where Jason beat his mother before strangling her to death. Jason later admitted he tried to scrub the stains out of the carpet before giving up and covering them with a white throw rug.
(*Courtesy Orange County Sheriff's Department*)

The Dumpster at the Oceanside housing complex where Jason and Matthew tried to discard their mother's remains.
(*Courtesy Orange County Sheriff's Department*)

and watched downloaded TV shows. No one ever said anything to Jason about it.

"He certainly didn't have any faculty members looking
over his shoulder or anything," Mantei said. "He could
have come in at night and downloaded porn all night long
if he wanted to and we'd never know."

As it turns out, Jason used the extra computer time to
download music and computer games. He knew ways to
download copies of television shows, too, including *That
'70s Show*, *Alias*, *King of the Hill*, and *The X-Files*. Then
he simply burned them to discs and took them all home to
watch with Matthew.

His favorite download was the HBO mega-hit *The
Sopranos*, a show that chronicled the ups and downs
of modern-day mob life in New Jersey. At the time, the
show was lauded by critics for its involving, realistic
story lines, but slammed for its powerfully graphic violence. Episodes included scenes of a mobster dragging
his pregnant stripper girlfriend into an alleyway and brutally kicking and beating the life out of her. One showed
the vicious rape of another character. Every season fans
watched as favorite characters got "whacked" (killed) for
grievances big and small.

Friends stopped short of saying that Jason was obsessed with the show, but he certainly loved it. And he
never missed an episode, including one called "Whoever
Did This."

In what would become one of the most infamous *Sopranos* episodes ever shot, lead character Tony Soprano
gets into a verbal argument with fellow henchman Ralphie Cifaretto over a racehorse. The fight escalates until
Tony pummels his pal to death. In a supposedly classic
mob move, Tony and his cousin drag their dead associate

to a nearby bathtub where they cut off his head, then saw off the hands, before dumping the body. The move is supposed to make it nearly impossible for cops to identify the corpse, should it ever accidentally be discovered.

Jason recorded the episode at school, then watched it on his home computer with Matt. According to Matt, the two watched the episode multiple times. But that wasn't particularly unusual—they often re-watched their favorite shows. In fact, they never talked about the episode at all. Matt could never have known then what kind of impact that show would later have on his brother and on their lives together.

With the extra income at the computer lab, Jason was now making pretty good money. He brought in about $1,000 a month at the Holiday Inn, and another $500 for the twenty hours a month he put in at the lab. With financial aid, he made about $24,000 a year. But he didn't think about leaving home now, mainly because Jane was actually doing all right.

She washed laundry, went to the grocery store, cooked dinner at night, and rarely talked about entertainment industry bad guys, Mexicans on the roof, Jews around the house, child molesters, Internet spies . . . Life was more normal than it had ever been in the Bautista household.

"I had no reason to leave," Jason said.

There were minor discomforts. After all, life with Jane was never entirely normal. She still refused to get any furniture out of storage. There were no mattresses in the two bedrooms. Instead, they slept in sleeping bags on the floor. They had a computer, but no Internet. A television, but no cable. No phones. No couches. Not even a refrigerator.

Still, to Matt and Jason, these were good times, and not even a bare house could change that.

Jane's beloved dog was still around, too—even though the lease on the Riverside place specifically forbade pets. Jason was always nervous that the animal would get them evicted. Though Jane mainly kept it in her room, it still needed to be taken out for walks. And there were times, at night, when it barked uncontrollably. Jason convinced his mother that the dog should spend some time at a kennel, to reduce their chances of getting caught. He knew if the family ever got evicted, it could trigger another stretch of homelessness. He wouldn't let that dog come between him and a home. Jane was reluctant. She still loved the dog deeply. But ultimately she drove the animal several nights a week to a boarding kennel in Moreno Valley.

It's not clear what Jane did all day while her sons were at school. She had no friends, never spoke to her neighbors, didn't work, and rarely went outside alone. But, to her sons, she seemed content for the moment. And they were grateful simply for that.

Meanwhile Matt settled into his new school. Despite the chaos of homelessness, he had earned a 3.2 overall GPA while home-schooled. But during his first semester back, his grades plummeted to a 1.7 average. Certainly, it couldn't have been easy re-adjusting to the rigors of a structured schedule. But there was likely another reason for the sliding GPA. Fifteen-year-old Matt made fast friends at school. And soon, he wasn't coming straight home after classes. Often, he lingered to hang out with his new buddies, sometimes to drink, sometimes to smoke pot. Smoking pot became a regular part of Matt's routine—he acknowledged as much in interviews with investigators and in court. It helped him zone out from the problems at home. Gone were the days of playing sports, excelling at hockey and golf. It was easier to escape with friends through after-school parties. Though things were quieter now—especially since his brother was gone so much, working two jobs and going to school—home was never a pleasant place to be.

Though Matt seemed very well liked at school, one afternoon he ended up in a campus fistfight. School administrators broke it up and told him he'd have to call his parents to pick him up. With no home phone, he couldn't call Jane, and he didn't want to, anyway. No telling how she would react. Instead, he called his big brother. Jason was working one of his rare afternoon shifts at the hotel and turned to Dan for permission to leave.

"That was Jason, always taking care of business," Dan said. "He would have done anything for his little brother."

Jason took off immediately to retrieve his sibling. Lately, Jason had taken on more of a fatherly role in Matt's life. He made sure homework was done and that Matt got up for class every day. And when Matt got in trouble, Jason went to campus and dealt with school administrators.

"Don't worry," he told them. "My mom works all day and couldn't come. But I'll tell her everything. Matt won't go unpunished."

In truth, Jason told her nothing. That meant one more day of normalcy. Instead, he talked to Matt directly. "Don't mess this up for us," he said. "You want to set her off? You've got to straighten up."

Matt's slipping grades and pot use continued, but he never got into another fight.

• • •

Jason continued to excel at school. Though he still carried the "geek" reputation that had earned him so much grief in high school, as a biochemistry major in college, he saw a lot of students just like himself—too smart for their own good.

"He was just a chemistry dork like the rest of us," said friend Sarah Reinelt, who met Jason in September 2002 in a biology class. She remembers first seeing him, clad in jeans, a plaid shirt, a pair of black-rimmed glasses, and bulky, silver Nike shoes ("I always told him they looked like moon shoes," Sarah said). To the bubbly and outgoing college coed, he always seemed a little out of place—but Sarah found this endearing. She was drawn to the overgrown awkward guy and ended up spending a lot of time working in the computer lab, where Jason often helped her with class projects.

"He was kind of a computer dork, that's for sure," Sarah joked. "He'd always talk about computers. He'd say, 'Oh, I got a new modem,' or RAM or some bullshit like that. He loved computers and video games."

Sarah was a year behind Jason and routinely turned to him for assistance. Sometimes, he even slipped her the answers to past tests, since some professors were in the habit of using the same exams year after year. The two became fast friends. In fact, Sarah always knew about the crush he developed toward her. But the pretty, petite blond coed had a boyfriend. Sarah didn't "feel like that" about Jason, she admitted.

"But I liked him," Sarah said. "I just thought he was a cool guy. We used to ditch class and go get lunch together and just laugh. I even had him over to my house. He's had dinner with my family."

Jason rarely talked about his home life. But Sarah suspected things were not good. He mentioned helping out with bills at home because his mom had trouble working. But more telling, Sarah said, was Jason's mood one night after dining with her and her mom.

"Man, your family is so cool," he kept telling Sarah. And in a way, the admission made her sad for him.

"Because you could just tell, the way he said it," Sarah said. "You could tell he totally wanted that. He wanted a family."

Sarah's mom was clearly taken with Jason, too. He was polite, articulate, ambitious, and obviously adored her daughter.

"You ought to date that boy," she told Sarah.

Mostly Sarah remembered being impressed with Jason because, though a young man just turned 20, he already had his entire future planned.

"He talked about the future all the time," Sarah said. "He just couldn't wait. I thought it was so cool to hear him talk like that. He was going to get his bachelor's degree in biochemistry, then go on to law school and become a biochemistry lawyer. He talked about how, you know, big firms like Marlboro have to have lawyers with a scientific background so they can defend their lawsuits, that type of thing. That's what he wanted to do. He had it all laid out. That's why it's such a shame what happened. He had so much he wanted to do with his life. I still can't believe it."

16

"Things were good," Jason told investigators after his arrest for murdering his mother. The first four months in the apartment in Riverside were some of the best times the family ever had together. Jane took them to the movies, cooked dinner almost every night, was concerned about Matthew's grades. She even stopped fighting with Jason, though, in truth, he spent fewer and fewer hours at home because of his hectic work and school schedule. But when he was home, life was stable.

"I liked living there, it was great," Jason said. "My mom was, like, nice again. And everything was cool. She wasn't crazy. It was, like, well, things were going really well. And then she just . . . I don't know. Something triggered it again."

"The man next door is a pedophile," Jane told Jason one October afternoon. The statement was like a punch in the stomach. Not because he believed her, but because he knew what was coming. Her sickness was raising its ugly head. He just couldn't bear the thought of enduring any more.

"I saw him in the paper," she continued. "The maintenance man is in on it, too. They've been trying to break into our house to get Matt."

Jason tried to shut her out. He turned his attention to the TV and stared intently at the screen.

"I've seen the man upstairs sitting in his car, too. He sits there for hours at a time, just watching me. He's going to come get me and get Matthew, too."

Jason shook his head and told her, "No, no, you're wrong, Mom. He doesn't want to hurt you or Matthew."

"Are you a molester, too?" she asked. "Do you molest your little brother when I'm gone?"

"No! No, of course not," he said. He knew it was her illness talking now, and there would be no reasoning with her.

Over the weeks, her delusions continued. Now, she thought people were breaking into the house to hide cameras everywhere.

"We're on videotape for the whole world to see!" she screamed one night. "Don't you care? Don't you even care at all? Or are they paying you again? Now you're being paid and you're against me and you're going to get me, too!"

At first, Jason coped by staying gone even longer, picking up extra graveyard shifts at the hotel and spending more time with friends. He hoped she'd snap out of it. But after several weeks, it was the same thing.

"Listen to that," Jane laughed to Matt one evening while watching late night TV. "Jay Leno is making fun of you!"

Sometime in late November, fearful of what was coming, Jason told Matt they needed to make a decision.

"I won't be homeless again," he said. He was certain his little brother understood what he was getting at. He waited for Matt's reaction. There was none, so he continued.

"Can't you see what's coming? I can't move again. It'll mess everything up for me. I can't study or go to work. It's too much stress. Matt, we've got to stop her this time. I think I'm just going to do it. But I need your help."

It's still hard to understand why Jason thought of murder before he considered trying to move out again. He even had a second job this time. He could have spent a few weeks saving up, and then just walked away. But for some reason, known only to him, murder became the more attractive option. Obviously, the thought had to have occurred to him—if she were gone, who would miss her? She had no friends, rarely talked to her family. Only Matt would know. And if Jason could get him involved, Matt would be an accomplice, so why would he tell anyone? Plus, those monthly $1,500 checks from Grandma would keep on coming. Jason endorsed them most of the time anyway and deposited them to the joint account he shared with Jane. Life could just go on, but without the constant threat of her mental meltdowns.

Matt remained quiet, listening to his brother hint at murdering their mother. Matt still didn't believe Jason would do it. Not really. This was probably just more of his talk.

"But the thing is," Jason pushed on, "she's really strong. So I'm going to need your help. I need you to hold her down."

"No way," said Matt, suddenly taking his brother more seriously. Matt was every bit as scared of returning to the streets as Jason. And he knew their mom was spiraling downward again. He thought about the options for a moment, then told his brother, "Listen, holding her down and all that, that's your thing, okay? I can't do it."

But if his brother could actually pull it off, Matt decided he would not stand in Jason's way. That was good enough for Jason.

"Okay," Jason said. "This is what's going to happen.

I'm going to bait her, get her mad and really heated. Then she'll get real violent and I'll just fight back this time. And Matt . . ."

"Yeah?"

"When that starts to happen, you walk away. Just leave or go into another room for a while or something. Okay?"

"Okay."

Matt didn't know when, exactly, it would happen. In fact, he still doubted that his brother had the guts to do it. But at school and at work, Jason clearly had Jane on his mind.

Biology classmate and lab partner Stephen Kavousy remembered Jason talking more and more about his mom. He complained about her a lot, which was odd because up until then, Jason had rarely mentioned her at all.

"She doesn't even work," Jason confided to Stephen. "And that makes it pretty damn hard for me because I end up working more and more to support her and my brother."

Still, Stephen remembered thinking that Jason seemed pretty upbeat as the winter semester began in early January. Odd, he thought, considering the heavy course load his friend was carrying (math 120, biology, and, one of the most difficult courses a science major must master, physical chemistry). Maybe Jason only *seemed* in high spirits because, as he worked through lab assignments, Stephen noticed, his pal was constantly singing. Stephen could never place the tune sung over and over in class. He'd never heard it before. But Jason was certainly fond of the song.

"It always amazes me how I can kill a man and it doesn't faze me," Jason sang repeatedly. As he pored over books and tinkered with lab assignments, the tune burst from Jason's lips: "It always amazes me how I can kill a man and it doesn't faze me."

Stephen didn't give the lyric too much thought. It was only later, in retrospect, that the song's eerie message made sense.

On the morning of January 14, 2003, Jason showed up early to the Cal State–San Bernardino campus for a study group. He had a biology test later that day and needed to be prepared. Later, he moved on to the computer lab to help some younger students with equations. After a long day of studying and working at the lab, Jason grabbed some dinner out of a nearby vending machine and then drove home. He made it to the Riverside apartment just before 7 p.m.

Jason dropped his book bag to the floor and sat in front of the TV, intent on zoning out for a little while. Matt was there, fooling around with a game on the computer. Jane cooked some pasta in the kitchen. For nearly ten minutes, all was quiet.

Then Jane started. It was the man upstairs, again.

"He's a pedophile, Jason," she said. "His picture is even in the paper. I'll prove it! I'll get it for you and show you!"

"Yeah, right," Jason said. "Just leave me alone. I really don't want to hear it tonight."

"I'll prove it to you! I can prove it! I've seen him in the paper!" she screamed.

"It doesn't matter what you do," Jason told her. "I don't believe you. You don't know anything, so stop. The man's not a pedophile, he's just a man. Do you understand me? I don't believe you!"

Jason knew he shouldn't have said that unless he was ready for a fight. It was the thing that set Jane off the

most—to be told she wasn't believed. It was openly ex-
pressed disbelief that had caused Jason to end up with a
hockey stick upside the head a few years ago. Jane's rage
grew, prompting her to scream even louder.

"How do you think this man makes money, huh?" she
asked. "They pay him! I've seen him digging through the
trash all the time."

"Just leave the man alone! He didn't do anything!"

"Oh, I see," Jane said. "It's you. You're the one being
paid. You're against me, huh? You're watching us. The
whole conspiracy has you now, doesn't it? Well, I'm not
going to stand for this. You're out of here!"

She stormed into Jason's room, grabbed a large blue
suitcase, and furiously tossed his clothes into it.

"You can't throw me out," he yelled back. "I'm on the
lease!"

"Oh yes I can! Just watch me," she said, continuing to
pack. "I can do whatever I want!"

"Fine, you want me out, that's fine," Jason yelled. He
helped fill the suitcase, throwing in his boxer shorts and
socks.

As the fight grew louder, more intense, Matt put down
his video game and went into his mother's room and
closed the door. Her dog was there, kept in her bathroom.
Matt sat with it for a good ten minutes, stroking its ears
and trying to take his mind off the chaos erupting in the
next room. But it was a tiny apartment. There was no es-
caping their angry words. With the fight clearly audible,
Matt moved the dog into the bedroom, flipped on the television, and turned up the volume. He focused on the
small screen, concentrating hard enough to block out the
heated voices just beyond the bedroom door. Another
fifteen rage-filled minutes clicked by. Jane told Jason his

grades weren't good enough, that he needed to be home more, that he needed to work more . . . Jason screamed back, mostly calling her crazy.

Then Matt heard it. A very loud thump, like someone had just hit the ground.

Still, Matt stayed put. Whatever was going on out there, he didn't want to know. He looked at the door leading to the living room, but didn't go near it. He'd seen them fight so many times, he didn't want to watch it now. He was sick of it. But it was more than that. He knew very well that tonight, right now, in fact, Jason just might be acting on his plan. If so, he didn't want to watch that, either. That was Jason's business. Instead, he remained frozen in front of his mom's old 13-inch television, gripping the dog tightly.

Jason stood in the middle of his tiny living room looking down at the lifeless body of his mother.

The last few minutes were a blur, but he knew what he had just done. He'd killed her. As she'd lashed out at him, her face red with rage, he'd finally knocked her to the floor, then grabbed her, hard, around the throat and choked the life out of her.

He stood still for a minute, maybe two, before turning to get Matt. He clicked the knob leading into Jane's bedroom and poked his head inside the doorway. Matt was there, on the floor, dog nearby. Though the TV was on, Matt was staring in his brother's direction.

"What happened?" Matt asked.

Jason just looked at his little brother. He wasn't ready to say it yet, but he didn't have to. Matt understood. Jason had finally killed their mother. It was hard to believe, but he knew it was true. Mom was dead and his brother was her murderer. He should have cried or felt some sadness at the news, but he didn't. If he felt any emotion at all, he showed no sign of it. Maybe after years of enduring the insane life his mother's madness had induced, he'd become too accustomed to dealing with pain. By now, he'd grown cold to it.

"Come out here and check her," Jason said. His hair was disheveled, his voice flat, monotone. He appeared calm.

Matt stepped into the living room and saw his mom lying very still, facedown on the floor. There were no tears or hysterics. This was his mother, and he'd grown to love her. But she was a brutal woman and the simple truth was that life would be mercifully quieter without her.

"Check her pulse," Jason ordered. "See if she's breathing."

Matt rolled her over. He picked up her arm, but he knew already. "Dude, she's dead."

"I know," Jason said. "I guess I already knew that."

"Well, now what?" Matt asked. "Now what happens?"

Jason took a deep breath, then answered, "We're going to have to take care of it, just like the Sopranos," he said.

Matt knew exactly what Jason meant. The gruesome episode flashed through his mind, the scene of Tony Soprano and his nephew slicing off victim Ralphie's head and hands. He shuddered.

"That's horrible," he said. "I can't do that."

"I know it's horrible, but what else are we going to do? We have to get rid of the body," said Jason. He didn't even know what he was going to do with the head and hands after he severed them. But he'd think about that later. Right now he just wanted to dump the body, and without a head or fingerprints, he knew the remains would be almost impossible to identify. Still, the task at hand was a gruesome one. Jason began to cry. "Dude, I just want to kill myself."

"Don't," Matt answered. "Please don't. I need you."

Jason took a few minutes to pull himself together, then he ordered Matt back to Jane's room. He fell into big brother/quasi-father mode and decided to shelter Matt from the worst of it. "Just stay there until I come and get you."

"I need to get out of here," Matt answered. "I'm going to go outside and grab a smoke."

Jason knew his brother didn't mean a cigarette. Getting high had become Matt's favorite coping mechanism of late.

"Okay, but don't be gone too long," Jason said.

Matt couldn't wait to be in the cool night air. He tried to visit his neighbor and classmate who lived in the complex and often had a joint to share. But he wasn't home, so Matt walked the complex alone and settled for puffing on a cigarette. Lots of thoughts crossed his mind as he tried to absorb the reality of the situation—Jason had finally killed Mom.

As he mulled it all over, he never thought of calling the police. Jason was all he had now. If he went to prison, Matt would be alone. As he walked, Matt knew he would protect Jason as much as he could. He needed his big brother, now more than ever.

Resolute in what he was about to do, Jason drove to the grocery store for supplies: rubber gloves, trash bags, a gallon of bleach, some Mountain Dew, and a pack of gum. When he returned, Jason took everything to the bathroom he shared with Matt and carefully laid his purchases out on the counter. He then searched the house for the family's boxed kitchen knife set. It was brand-new, with most of the knives still wrapped in plastic and a $19.99 sale price sticker still on the box. Jason withdrew the large butcher knife and a pair of shearing scissors, placing them on the bathroom counter with the rest of his supplies.

Back in the living room, Jason bent to scoop up his mother's corpse. She was a heavy woman now, having lost all interest in her appearance and figure years ago, so he struggled to drag her 170-pound frame toward the bathroom. Once there, he took a few minutes to disrobe her, down to her panties.

He could hear Matt returning home and stepped out to greet him. Matt was startled to see his brother clad only in boxer shorts and a tank top.

"Stay out of our bathroom," Jason told him.

"Okay," Matt answered, not pushing for any more information. Instead, he headed back to Jane's room, stepping over the small blood spatters staining the beige living room carpet. He flipped on the television and waited.

Jason returned to the bathroom, eager to get his gruesome task over with. He grabbed Jane's body, throwing her waist over the bathtub's edge, so her legs dangled out and her face touched the tub's inner wall. She hung there while Jason picked up a handful of that fiery red hair and chopped off a large chunk with the shearing scissors, leaving the neck clearly exposed. Tossing the strands to the floor, Jason reached for the butcher knife. He began to saw. As the blood spilled from her neck, Jason scurried to the toilet and threw up. He retched until his stomach was empty, then returned to his work and continued to cut.

• • •

Hours passed before Jason went to his little brother again. Matt was startled to see Jason's appearance. He looked like he'd been up for days. His hair was wild, his eyes blood-shot, and he was wearing a pair of gray slacks and dress shoes. Matt didn't know what to say to Jason. He wasn't eager to know the details of their mother's death and disposal.

"Come on, we've got to go," he said. "I need you to help me."

Matt stood to leave when Jason turned to him again and pointed to the dog Jane loved so much. "And bring him," he said.

Jason drove aimlessly for a while. The winter night sky was blissfully dark as the car hummed along. Neither brother spoke as they sat in that car, its trunk heavy with the weight of their mother's mutilated remains. Jason had used his sleeping bag to cover her body, rolling her in tightly before depositing her into the Oldsmobile.

As they drove, one of the boys flipped on the radio, aching to fill the heavy silence.

Jason's mind whirled, desperate to come up with a plan. He should probably dig a hole in some remote corner of the county. But he didn't have a shovel. He'd have to dump her somewhere. But where?

Well, at least he knew what to do with that damn dog. So he'd take care of that first. He drove to a kennel in nearby San Ysidro, one the family used now and then to board the dog. It was after midnight, so no one was there to take it. But Jason didn't care about that.

"What are we doing?" Matt finally asked.

"We've got to get rid of him, Matt," Jason said. "He's causing too many problems."

He gladly pulled the canine from the car and quickly drove away. He knew and loved the dog, too, but to Jason, it was just another reminder of the mother he was extinguishing from his life. Anyway, they could be evicted if anyone discovered the dog. And nothing would ever again put his stability in jeopardy.

Jason got back on the freeway and headed south, toward San Diego County. Nearly an hour passed before he pulled off the freeway and into the city of Oceanside, where the family had lived with Matt's dad so many years ago. They drove toward a housing tract, slowly passing the well-kept homes aligning upscale Saint Malo Beach's sandy shoreline. Abruptly, he stopped the car in front of a two-story home on South Pacific Street. The Oldsmobile's headlights illuminated a huge Dumpster that sat in front of a home clearly undergoing some renovations.

"That's it," Jason said. "Let's do it here."

Though Matt never asked Jason what they were doing, he knew. They got out, silently, and pulled at the edges of Jason's dark brown sleeping bag. But as they walked toward the Dumpster, a voice cut the night's silence. They froze and looked up at the advancing frame of security guard Pete Martinez.

Trying to stay as calm as possible, despite a wildly beating heart, Jason took a hard look at Pete. He was in uniform, but Jason doubted this old man was a cop. He was just a security guard. He couldn't arrest them. He couldn't do anything. The boys yanked on the bag again, intent on returning it to the trunk. But suddenly, the old man began barking orders.

"Hey! Stop! Put the bag down!" he shouted, reaching for a pistol at his side.

Instantly, Jason turned from frightened to pissed-off.

"Fuck you! You're just a security guard! You can't do anything," he said. They tossed Jane into the trunk and sped off, never realizing Pete knew they were hauling more than a load of leaves and branches. He knew because he had seen the foot.

Jason trembled behind the wheel as he drove away. The night had left him totally drained, emotionally and physically. He headed back onto the 5 Freeway, intent on heading home and leaving the body in the trunk of the car until morning. He turned off onto the 74 Freeway, also known as the Ortega Highway. He knew that road would eventually take him to Highway 215, through his old stomping grounds in Menifee and on to Riverside. As he drove the Ortega, he realized that he was alongside a steep cliff. It was about 2 a.m., and the road was nearly deserted. Maybe this was the place to do it. He pulled over to a rest stop and got out.

"Just stay here, Matt," Jason said. Matt nodded before reclining his seat all the way back and closing his eyes. He was exhausted, too.

Jason scooped up the bag from the trunk. As he stood on the cliff's edge, he lifted Jane out of the bag, deciding even that might be too much evidence to leave behind. He pushed her nearly naked remains as hard as he could off the edge. Even drained of blood, missing head and hands, she was so heavy that the shove unbalanced him. He slipped and, for a moment, thought he'd follow her down that hill. But he didn't. He regained his balance and watched the body roll until it disappeared down the dark hillside. He looked at his gray dress pants and saw they were now ruined, smeared with Jane's blood. He'd thought for sure most of her blood had already flowed down the bathtub drain. Part of him felt sick inside. But he tried not to focus on that. Because this was his moment. Finally, he was free. And nobody could take that from him now.

Once home, the boys went to Jane's room and slept. Despite his exhaustion, it was a fitful night for Jason. He finally gave up around 5 a.m. and decided to take care of some details. He grabbed a bunch of trash bags and gathered up the clothes his mom had worn, his dress shoes and pants, the sleeping bag, the strands of hair he'd cut from Jane, and his rubber gloves. It was still dark out when he drove to Hemet, a few cities over, and tossed them into a Dumpster behind a mini-mart. When he returned home, Matt was awake.

"You should go to school today," Jason told him. "Just because she's not here doesn't mean you don't have to go to school."

While Matt was at school, Jason set about cleaning up the apartment. He scrubbed at the bloodstains on the carpet, but they wouldn't come out. He'd buy a large throw rug later and cover them up, he decided. He drenched the bathroom with bleach and cleaned until every spot of blood disappeared. Satisfied, he reached for his backpack and left for afternoon classes.

17

Orange County Sheriff's Investigator Andre Spencer had been with the homicide unit for nearly three years. And he loved it.

"The best thing I get to do is put a murderer in jail," Spencer liked to say. "There's nothing better."

It brought him closer than most people ever wanted to get to tragedy. But the 36-year-old detective didn't find that depressing. Because he didn't focus on the tragedy. His job was to find the justice. It was the only way to look at his role in law enforcement and not get jaded. After participating in roughly thirty murder investigations, the married father of three didn't want to remember all those wasted lives when he was home coaching his kids' soccer teams. It was easier to think about the small comfort the victims' families got when the bad guy, his bad guy, went to prison forever.

It was about 8:30 a.m. when Orange County Sheriff's Homicide Sergeant Bill Vining approached Andre's desk. Apparently, a citizen heading west on the Ortega Highway thought they'd seen a body.

"Hey," he announced to the half-dozen or so homicide detectives working away at their desks. "Looks like we have a body dump."

Everyone moved to put on their jackets and head for the scene. When a murder breaks, it's "all hands on deck." But the job of lead detective rotates. Andre knew what was coming. He was next on the list.

"Andre," Vining said, "this one's going to be yours. Should be interesting. It's a woman. She has no hands, no head."

He grimaced. Not only because of the gruesomeness of the crime. He was used to gruesome in this business. But it was going to be hard as hell to get an ID on this woman, who had no head for dental records, no hands to run fingerprints. Well, he'd get a set of criminalists out there ASAP to do whatever they could. They could still swab the corpse to get a DNA sample. And if she had been sexually assaulted, there might be semen.

Andre was a tall, muscular guy. He liked to spend several hours a week at the gym, sweating out the stresses of homicide work. He was a black man with light coffee-colored skin, and kept his head shaved clean. When he wanted to, he could cut quite an intimidating picture to an interview subject. But in truth, Andre Spencer was a gentle man, genuinely respected by others in his department.

As he drove to the scene, Andre's cell phone chirped. "Spencer here," he said.

It was Sergeant Vining. Apparently, a homeless guy had been detained for breaking into a ranger station just up the road from the corpse.

Andre was thinking of the Stephanie Crowe case from the 1990s. A 12-year-old girl had been brutally stabbed to death in her San Diego home. Her mom and dad were there at the time, asleep, as were her grandmother and 14-year-old brother. All of them were questioned. But as it turned out, a transient traveling through the area had killed her.

"Shit, this could be our guy, you know," Andre said.

"Anyway, it sounds promising. I'm on my way."

But once there, Spencer changed his mind. Investigators said the transient was cold, hungry, and wanted somewhere to sleep. But he swore he'd had nothing to do with the body up the road. Andre didn't believe this was the guy. Just a gut feeling.

To be on the safe side, Investigators Gary Jones and Toni Bland picked up the transient and took him to the jail, where they got hair samples, took his picture, and booked him on the burglary charge. Meanwhile, Spencer quickly moved on to the crime scene in search of answers.

"Jesus, this is awful," said Investigator Craig Johnson, Andre's partner and, therefore, second in command of the investigation. Craig was standing at the bottom of the ravine, wearing a pair of rubber gloves. Craig's 6'4" frame loomed over the nearly naked corpse. She had on a bloody pair of panties, nothing else. Clearly, someone had tossed her from the roadway's railing, now smeared with blood streaks. She'd tumbled ninety feet before coming to rest at the bottom of the hillside. Her body was so pale, the skin took on a ghostly white appearance.

"There's no blood in her," Craig said. "She wasn't just decapitated. For the body to be this dry, someone drained all the blood from her. That's pretty evident."

They surmised from her torso that the woman was about 5'7" tall, on the heavy side, probably around 160 pounds. Her skin was fair, so no doubt she was Caucasian. She was covered in a fine sheath of red body hair. A redhead. There was no animal activity, so she was otherwise intact. But that was it. After twelve hours of collecting the scarce evidence found at the scene—no weapons, no fibers—Craig helped the coroner's investigator lift the torso into a black body bag. Perched on the hill's bottom slope, Craig grabbed at her wrist and tugged. With no hand to stop his pull, his hand slid off. He looked at the blood smears he'd caught from brushing against her severed wrist.

"This is gross," he grumbled, then reached for the wrist again. Success.

The torso was tucked into a black body bag and sent off to the coroner's office for an autopsy. Now, Andre and Craig thought, on to finding the sick bastards who'd mutilated this woman. They'd have to search through missing persons reports. They'd have to blanket the media, doling out every detail they had on her appearance in hopes that something would ring a bell with someone.

"Anyone's mom, sister, best friend who hasn't been seen in a while but not reported missing yet," Spencer said. "That's what we're looking for."

Mostly, they prayed for a really good tip.

18

It was late afternoon, January 14, 2003, when Matt returned home from school. He grabbed a snack before flipping on the afternoon news. That's when he first heard about the discovery of Jane's body. According to the report, a motorist had spotted it as it lay at the bottom of that steep ravine along the Ortega Highway. The reporter noted that police were shocked at the brutality of the murder—the unidentified corpse had been beheaded and left without hands. Matt felt a kick in his gut. He'd asked so few questions the night before, he hadn't realized that Jason had actually gone through with cutting off their mom's head. For some reason, only now did he feel angry. He had to know what had happened. When Jason came home, he finally asked.

"Tell me what happened last night," Matt said.

"You don't need to know all of it," Jason told him.

"I want to know," Matt persisted.

"I did what I told you I was going to do," Jason replied.

"You killed her," Matt said.

"Yes, I killed her."

"Well, the police found her," Matt answered. "I saw a news report on TV about it. Dude, they said she didn't have a head. What the hell? How could you do it?"

"I did it so they couldn't identify her," Jason said. "So it'll be clean."

"Did you dump that stuff last night, too?"

"No," Jason said, "I didn't."

"Where are they?"

"In a duffel bag in the hall closet," Jason said. "So don't go in there. Don't touch it. I'm trying to figure out what to do with them."

Matt agreed. He didn't want to see that stuff anyway. It should have freaked him out to know they were standing just a few inches away from his mother's remains, but once again, he pushed the thought out of his mind.

"Listen, we need to know what to say if anyone asks about her," Jason said. "Hopefully no one will, since she didn't talk to anybody. But if anyone asks about your mom, you tell them she went out of town indefinitely. Tell them she went to Chicago or she ran off to Belize to be with some guy she met on the Internet or something like that."

"Okay," said Matt. He didn't know how to feel about everything. He'd never been treated as badly as Jason had. He'd grown to love his mother, even though he'd hated her sickness. He was only 15, not ready to lose the only mom he'd ever known. He wasn't mad at Jason, really. Mostly, he felt scared. "Jason, are we going to be okay?"

"Yes, it's going to be okay," Jason said. "But you have to help around here more, maybe. She's not here to cook or clean anymore. We have to do that. And you have to stay in school. You have to be successful one day, Matt. That means you have to study and stop screwing around. This is our chance to have a normal life. I did this for both of us. So don't mess it up."

The next week was blissfully quiet for the boys. And yes, happy. Jason drove to the storage units, where he unrolled a wad of cash to get the neglected account up to date, then brought home some furniture. He filled the empty apartment with beds, a couch, and a chair. He bought a large white rug and tossed it over the bloodstains. He bought cell phones, long forbidden by Jane, for himself and Matthew. He allowed Jason's friends over, where they played video games and just generally hung out.

But at least one person had questions regarding Jason's whereabouts. At the computer lab, Jason was scheduled for a 6 p.m. shift on January 14. The lab was closed to students that night so employees could do some upgrade work on the computers. A reminder for staffers was posted in large block letters on the blackboard. But Jason skipped it, too exhausted after the previous night's activities, and too caught up in details like bathroom cleanup and disposal of his mother's belongings. He didn't even call in to offer an excuse. So, when Jason strolled in two nights later, Supervisor Kenneth Poarch was clearly irritated.

"What happened to you?" Poarch said. "You know we were counting on you."

"Yes, I know," Jason said, putting on his best aw-shucks act. "It's just, oh man, well, my girlfriend," he stammered. "She called and said we had to have dinner with her parents. It was a real spur-of-the-moment, last-minute thing. And I've never met her parents before, so I kind of had to go. But I'm so sorry."

"Fine, don't let it happen again," Poarch said, clearly not happy with Jason's irresponsibility. Still, he was generally a good kid and a reliable employee. Since it had never happened before, Poarch let the incident slide.

Christian Revecho could be gone for really long stretches, thanks to his job as a truck driver. But on January 20, 2003, he was home, staring out his living room window.

He watched as his young neighbors, Matt and Jason, took several trips between their apartment and the Dumpster, carrying huge bulging trash bags.

From inside the apartment, Jason organized the systematic removal of all things related to Jane Bautista. Mostly, he wanted her clothes out of his closet. Now that she was gone, Jason decided to move into the apartment's master bedroom for good. He hung a few movie posters. And in his final act of rebellion, he bought a bumper sticker bearing the phrase "BADA BING!," the name of the strip club owned by Tony Soprano. He peeled off the sticker's backing and firmly attached it to the rear of his new car, the Oldsmobile.

Friends noticed more profound changes with the two boys. Mainly, both now freely invited people over.

Friend Stephen Kavousy said it was a couple of weeks before Super Bowl Sunday when he chatted with Jason in biology lab. "Hey, I'm going to have some people over to watch the game. Why don't you come?"

Steven was shocked by the invitation.

"Well, my mom finally left town," Jason said excitedly. "And she left me the new car!"

Matt had friends in and out of the apartment all the time, too—especially a young girl he had a huge crush on. One afternoon, as Matt and the girl hung out at the apartment after school, she gave him a brown teddy bear. He propped the little toy up on his bed, where he would keep it each day.

It could be said that Matt was just a typical adolescent boy, lost in a teenage infatuation. It could, except that just a few feet away from that bear, in the hall closet, lay a horrific reminder of just how abnormal life had become.

19

Andre Spencer pored over his latest clue sheet—the log that dispatchers used to record tips as they came in from the public. The media had done a great job of picking up the story. A headless, handless female torso found thrown from the side of a busy freeway? That's a story so grisly, it's tailor-made for nightly news headlines. Andre waded through the more than 100 tips that had come in. Most were useless—friends looking for a lost woman with a tattoo or dark hair. Someone even called in wondering if it could be a lost African American friend. Andre steadily crossed off anything that looked worthless.

It was the morning of January 21, a Tuesday, and Andre was antsy to catch a break in the case. Six days since the body had been discovered. In the world of homicide investigation, when every moment counts, six days was practically an eternity. But with little to go on, there was little to do. Andre took off Sunday and Monday to recharge his batteries by coaching his kids' soccer team. It was the heart of soccer season and he didn't want to miss out. He took the time to listen to his wife's latest adventures at work, too. She was an elementary school teacher. But Andre never mentioned his nameless homicide victim.

Long ago, Andre had made a promise to himself. "I don't bring it home," he says. "We're too busy with our kids and our lives to bring stuff like that home."

The time off was a much-needed break after long
discussions with Los Angeles County criminalist Steve
Dow, a specialist in dismemberment cases. Dow can look
at a cut and get a pretty good idea what kind of blade was
used to do the deed. This job wasn't too hard: it was a
clean cut, so it was likely just a large knife with a smooth
blade, he concluded. Good to know, but for now, it didn't
identify the victim, or bring Andre any closer to his
killer.

Andre continued reading down the tip list. His eyes
lingered on the name Pete Martinez. The man, a security
guard in San Diego County, had apparently called the tip
in last week. It had taken a few days for his story to cross
county jurisdictions and land in front of Andre. According to the log, Mr. Martinez had caught a couple of guys
trying to dump something, and in the process, thought
he'd seen a foot slip out of their bundle. Then Andre saw
the license plate number. What the hell, he thought.
There's nothing else to go on. Let's run it through the Department of Motor Vehicles.

It didn't take long to find the name the license plate
number was registered to. Actually two names. Jason
Bautista, an innocent-looking kid with glasses and brown,
spiky hair streaked with blond highlights. According to
his license, Jason was a big guy, standing 6'2" tall and
weighing 210 pounds. With that kind of size, he was certainly physically capable of manhandling a woman.

Then the next picture came up. A woman, Jane Bautista.
And she had red hair. Andre felt his stomach leap. This was
the victim, he just knew it. Other information fit, too—she
was 5'7" tall, 145 pounds.

He needed to find Jason Bautista, fast. But he hit another stumbling block. The address on both licenses was

a post office box in San Marcos. Craig thought about what to do next. Investigators would have to go to San Marcos and blanket the area with pictures of Jason, hoping someone would recognize him. In the meantime, Andre wanted to talk to Pete.

"This looks good," Andre confided in his partner, Craig Johnson. "Let's get out to him and see if he recognizes the license photo of Jason."

The detectives met Pete at his Oceanside home on January 23. They were impressed with Martinez. He was no crackpot. This was an honest guy, a Vietnam veteran.

"So, I've seen stuff like this before," he said. "Not in a long time, but you don't forget what that looks like. I've seen a lot of body bags in my time. That's what it looked like to me. Then the foot came out."

Andre nodded, then reached for Jason's license photo.

"Do you recognize this person?" he asked Pete.

"Yes," Pete said, without hesitation. "That's him! That's one of the guys, the big one, the one that did all the talking. The other one, the little sidekick, he never said a word."

"Okay," Andre said, suddenly wanting to get out of there and start tracking down an address for Jason Bautista. "You've been a big help. We'll be in touch."

Back at the office, Andre and Craig plugged Jason's name into multiple computer search engines, hoping to find some public record or criminal history for him, something that had a home address, family information, anything to go on. But Jason had no criminal record. Not even a traffic ticket. Investigators in San Marcos had also turned up empty. While they found neighbors who remembered the

Bautistas, it turned out Jane and Jason hadn't lived in that area for over six years.

It would be another two days before Andre got the break he'd been looking for. He ran Jason's name through the Employment Development Department, the state agency that issues unemployment checks. But the department also keeps track of who is working where to ensure that employees are paying into the system. Every working person must pay a tax to fund the unemployment program. According to their records, Jason was working for the InterContinental Hotels Group, which owns the Holiday Inn chain. Andre made a quick call to their headquarters and discovered that Jason was a desk clerk at the Holiday Inn in Ontario, California. Andre and Craig made the drive immediately.

As it turned out, it was Jason's day off. But Crystal Cantu told investigators they could find him at school. She even knew his schedule—physical chemistry, 1 p.m. No one at the hotel thought Jason was in any trouble. Clearly, something bad had happened. Spencer and Johnson had identified themselves as investigators in a missing persons case. Mostly, hotel staffers hoped Jason would survive whatever bad news he was about to get.

It was late morning, so Craig and Andre took an early lunch to kill time. Over lunch, Andre told Craig he didn't want to tell Jason about the body right up front.

"Let's just keep playing this up like we're working a missing persons case and see what he has to tell us," Andre said. "We'll just say somebody reported her missing. I have a hunch this kid could be a suspect, so I want to give him enough rope and see where he goes with it."

Craig nodded in agreement and the plan was set.

California State University was about a thirty-minute

drive from Ontario. The campus had its own police department, so the detectives decided to contact them first before finding Jason. An officer escorted them to Jason's classroom. Andre peeked inside and spotted Jason almost immediately.

"Hey, Jason," Andre whispered, causing him to snap his head toward the investigator's frame just inside the doorway. "Come out here, man. I need to talk to you for a second."

Jason scooped up his backpack and walked outside. Andre and Craig flashed their badges. Although they were in suits, they stood next to a uniformed campus officer. There's no telling what went through Jason's mind at that moment. Ice-cold fear must have flooded his stomach. He looked like such a kid, with his round, unlined face, dressed in a red-and-black plaid button-down shirt and baggy khaki pants, and clutching the strap of his backpack.

"Jason," Andre said, "can you come back to the campus police office so we can talk?"

"Yeah, sure. What about?" Jason said, trying to sound as casual as possible.

"I'll tell you more once we get to the office," Andre said.

Jason said nothing else. But the detectives could already see it—he was nervous. His face flushed red. And his eyes . . . "The eyes told me everything," Andre recalled. "He was scared."

At the police office, the men moved into a private conference room.

"Jason, we're investigating a missing persons case and we think maybe you can help us," Andre said. "So, we're going to ask you a few questions, okay?"

"Okay," Jason said warily.

The detectives secretly clicked on a recorder and turned their attention to Jason. They started slowly, asking him for his identification and a home address.

"You live there with who?" Spencer asked.

"My little brother and my mom, when she's there," Jason said.

"Well, like I said," Spencer told Jason, "we work in investigations. And there are some safety concerns for your mom."

"Yes," Jason said, but nothing more.

"Well, a friend of hers called and said she hasn't talked to her for a while. And they want us to try to locate her. So, basically, I need to know when you last saw her."

"She called me on Monday," said Jason, telling them that Jane had come home to let Jason have the Intrigue. "We switch cars occasionally. We also have a 'ninety-two Honda Accord Wagon."

"She has that one right now?"

"Yes, my mom should be in the Honda right now," Jason said. Matt, his little brother, wasn't with her, he added. Even though it was a school day, he had permission to go to Disneyland with friends.

"Okay, well, like we said, we're concerned for your mom's safety."

Jason was prepared for friends or co-workers asking about his mom. It was easy to tell them she was in Chicago. They wouldn't call family out there to verify the story. But cops would. Jason had to think fast, come up with another story.

"Well, she's in Corona with a boyfriend. She has a different boyfriend every freaking week," he said.

"What's his name?" Andre asked.

"I don't even know," Jason said. "She just tells us she's going to be gone for a while and then she calls, she checks in. I usually make sure all the bills are paid. And that's it . . . She meets all kinds of guys off the Internet."

"Where's her computer?" asked Andre, knowing they could search it and trace who she'd communicated with.

"I think she goes to Internet Cafe, because I don't want that going on at my house," Jason said. "I don't have Internet at my house because I took the modem out of our machine. She was on the Internet way too much."

He told detectives that Jane didn't work, she never had. Instead, she got money, up to $1,500, from her grandmother every month.

"Wow, that's pretty nice," Andre said. "You guys got it made, man!"

"She knows it's for me to get through college and Matt to get through high school," Jason said. "She loves us a lot."

"Okay, well, we're trying to find your mom, like I said. Could you describe her a little bit for me?"

"Oh, she's maybe five feet four inches tall," Jason lied. "Maybe one hundred and twenty pounds soaking wet."

The description was so different from the body discovered off the highway that Craig and Andre doubted themselves for a moment. Maybe they did have the wrong guy—though something deep down told them no, Jason was their man, and Jane was his victim. "Any scars or tattoos?"

"I know she has tattoos, I've seen them before," he lied again. "She has a sun on her back somewhere. It's like a sunburst and had some kind of pattern in the middle, then goes down in the middle. I know she's got Chinese characters done somewhere, too. One of her boyfriends is in tattooing."

The detectives knew Jason was lying. The body they had didn't have a mark on it. But they said nothing, continuing to listen as Jason related one deceptive detail after another.

"Wow, you guys seriously aren't joking, man," Jason added.

"No, we're not joking," Andre said. "We're trying to locate your mom . . . Where's your dad?"

"My father's deceased. It was a suicide."

"How do you get along with your mom?" Spencer asked.

"I love my mom," Jason shot back without hesitation. "Mom's great. Even though she doesn't work, she at least got our grandma to send us money. She's there when I need her to help me out. I love my mom."

"Any problems with your mom?"

"Except for her freaking boyfriends, no. No. No," Jason said. "She's just looking for a husband. But I mean, I don't get it. I told her she doesn't need one."

"Does she have any problems with relatives?" Andre asked.

"My grandma is an alcoholic. My grandfather is, too," Jason claimed, clarifying that all of their relatives were in Illinois, so he never saw them anyway. "But, like, our great-grandma, she's great. She's the one who helps us out. That's who I think of as my grandparent, because my real grandparents suck."

"Has she ever had problems with the neighbors?" Andre continued.

"Um, she doesn't like people. She has some kind of racist views a little bit," Jason said. "Because of the experiences with my father."

"He was Hispanic, I take it," Andre said.

"Yes. She's just a racist, pretty much."

"Do you and Matt have the same father?"

"No," Jason said. "But he has anger management issues. He's a beater. We haven't seen him since I was about eight."

"Is your mom pretty demanding of you and your brother?"

"No," Jason lied again. "My mom just says, 'Go to school, go to work, and we'll make it through.' She says that when I get my degree, we'll all be happy because we'll have a big house and I'll make lots of money."

"Do you know how to get ahold of your mom?" Andre asked.

"No, she usually calls us."

"When was the last time you physically saw her?" Craig wanted to know.

"I'm thinking last Thursday," he said. "That sounds about right. She was home like an hour. We went to dinner and then she left."

Craig was certain Jason was being deceitful, so he decided to press for every detail, hoping to make Jason as nervous as possible.

"Where did you have dinner?" Craig asked.

"At HomeTown Buffet."

"Which one?"

"In Moreno Valley at the mall," said Jason, smoothly spitting out answers as quickly as Craig threw questions at him.

"That was Thursday the sixteenth?"

"Yeah."

They continued to grill him, forcing him to explain

where he was the night before and the night before that, with who and for how long. Jason stammered, he got confused.

"I'm not sure of anything, just to be honest," Jason said. "I can't remember last week."

The detectives turned up the heat, sensing Jason might break soon. He was articulate, clearly a smart kid, and he knew it. Knew it so well, in fact, that he thought he could outtalk the detectives. Funny, it was kind of the same impression classmates of Jason's had had of him in high school—a cocky kid who wasn't nearly as smart as he thought he was.

"You know what?" Jason continued. "I think I might have some dates mixed up again. See, I'm just guessing at what I did, to be honest."

"Well, don't guess," Andre said. "We want to find out what you did, because our whole purpose is to find your mom."

"My mom will probably call tonight or tomorrow or soon," Jason offered. "I'll have her talk to you."

"We want to talk to her before that, Jason," Andre told him. He grew impatient with the dance, so he tried a more direct approach. "Do you go to Oceanside any?" he asked.

"When I was a child, we lived there."

"Recently, have you been to Oceanside?" Andre asked again.

"No, I have not been to Oceanside recently," he said.

"Do you let friends borrow your car?"

"No," he said. "It's either my mom in the car or, like, that's it."

"Okay, and you've never been to Oceanside in your car?" Andre said.

"No."

"Well, what if I tell you that I know for a fact that your car has been in Oceanside recently?" said Andre, watching Jason carefully for his reaction. He showed none.

"Then I'd ask why," Jason said.

"On Tuesday," Andre said. "We know that for a fact because a witness got the license plate."

"A witness to what?" Jason snapped.

"A witness to you being in Oceanside, dumping trash or something like that," Andre said.

"It wouldn't be me," he said.

"Jason," Craig cut in.

"Yes, sir?"

"Let's start being honest here," he advised Jason.

"I am being honest."

"No, you're not," Craig said simply. But Jason gave nothing more. "We didn't just start doing this, Jason, okay?"

"We know your car was in Oceanside," Andre added. "We know a lot . . . We have a witness that took that license plate down and we have a witness that saw you."

"Okay, well, it wasn't me," said Jason, refusing to let go of his lie. He wasn't ready to admit defeat, not yet, not when he was so close to a normal life. "I was not in Oceanside."

"What is Matthew going to tell us?" Andre asked.

"The same thing," Jason said.

"Jason, where is Matthew right now?" Craig asked.

"At Disneyland."

"Are you sure?" Craig pushed.

"Quite," he said.

"No, you're not," he said. "Are we talking to him right now? We didn't stop him on his way to Disneyland and start talking to him?"

"No. He's at Disneyland. If you guys can find him there . . . I mean, he would've called me if something was wrong."

"No, he wouldn't," Craig said. "Jason, you're lying about things, and we know it. You don't have a good relationship with your mother, we know you don't."

"How would you know I don't have a good relationship with my mother?" Jason snapped. Suddenly, he was angry. It was the first time he'd shown any emotion. "I don't care what other people say. My mom's important to me."

"What are the chances we show the witness the picture of your brother and he says, 'Well, that's the other guy'?" Craig asked.

"I don't know," Jason said.

"What are the chances?" Craig repeated.

"Should be zero."

"Well, what we need here is to locate your mom," Andre said. "Because we work missing persons. And we also work homicide."

"Homicide?" Jason repeated, incredulous.

"Yes, Orange County Sheriff's Homicide Division," said Andre, waiting for more reaction from Jason. There was none, so he continued. "And we can get a DNA profile on bodies. We can find their relatives by DNA. So, would you be willing to give a DNA swab of your mouth?"

Jason agreed and took a Q-tip offered to him, swabbed the end across the inside of his cheek, as instructed, and handed the sample back to Andre.

"Once again," Andre said, offering Jason one last chance to confess, "any idea where your mom is?"

"No."

"Okay," Craig said. "Jason, I think you're lying to me. We know more about what's going on than you think we know. We know quite a bit about what's going on. So, you're not under arrest, but we're going to detain you for a while. We're going to take your car, write a search warrant for it."

"Okay," Jason said calmly.

"And write a search warrant for your house," Craig added.

"Okay," he said, again, calmly. But on the inside, panic raged. His mother's head and hands. He'd never gotten rid of them.

The detectives stood, telling Jason they needed to step outside for a moment to make a few calls, then they'd be back to escort him to the sheriff's station.

"You hang on tight," Andre said. "We appreciate you helping us out on this, man. All of this will help us locate your mom."

"No problem."

As the door closed behind them, Jason reached for his cell phone and dialed Matt's number.

"Get away from home," Jason spat urgently into the phone. "Go somewhere else, do not come home. Stay away. Do it! Dude, do it!" Then he snapped the phone shut.

The detectives caught it all on tape, but Jason didn't know that then. As they walked back into the room, Andre saw Jason with the phone in his hand.

"Just checking your messages?" Andre asked.

"Yeah, just checking my voice mail."

Nearly an hour had passed since they'd begun talking. Certain they had the right suspect, Andre and Craig asked Jason to escort them to the Oldsmobile, currently parked on a lot inside the university campus. But Jason paused. Although he'd agreed to show them the car, he wasn't ready to do it. Not yet.

"I think I have something more to tell you," said Jason, realizing at last that he was in way over his head. Soon they would know everything. He had to get his side of the story out before he landed in jail.

"You ready to tell us what really happened?" Craig asked.

"Yes," Jason said. "I am."

20

Deputy District Attorney Michael Murray is the quintessential good guy. If this were the Old West, he'd don a ten-gallon cowboy hat, gleaming white. He's tall, with dark hair and dark eyes, and wickedly handsome. The 39-year-old prosecutor is a West Point Academy graduate who spent five years in the Army, leaving as a captain and intent on pursuing a law degree from the McGeorge School of Law in Sacramento, California. He married a woman in the FBI and has three little girls, all young enough to still need car seats. His sense of good versus evil is clearly defined. He is smart. He is moral. He is the ideal prosecutor.

Mike mulled over the call he'd just taken from Sergeant Vining. Of the 250 prosecutors in the district attorney's office, Murray was one of only seven handling the county's most serious crime—homicide. He took on any body discovered in the unincorporated parts of Orange County, as the Ortega Highway body had been. So it fell to Mike to write out the necessary search warrants for the Bautista apartment and get a judge to sign off on them.

But it occurred to Mike that the Orange County authorities may have been out of their jurisdiction. Sure, they had the body. But the suspect was from Riverside. In all probability, he'd committed the murder there, then crossed into Orange County to dump the remains. But

Mike wrote up the search warrants anyway. This was one case he didn't want to lose. It wasn't your run-of-the-mill bar fight, Mike thought. Already the press was calling like mad, desperate for any new details on the headless body case. And they didn't even know yet that the woman's sons might have been responsible. It would be fascinating to get to the bottom of this one, to know why a young man would so brutally mutilate the woman who'd given him life. So Mike settled into the case. Riverside police might have some rights to the case by jurisdiction, but Orange County investigators had the body, the defendants, and most of the facts. Until someone told Mike otherwise, this one belonged to him.

It was nearly 2:30 p.m. when Andre and Craig settled into their seats once again to listen to Jason's story. This time, Andre openly took out a tape recorder and set it on the small table in front of them.

"I'll just start," Jason said. "I'll tell you the story from the start. People are going to hate me. I didn't mean to . . ."

"Okay," said Andre in a calm, steady voice, hoping to keep Jason grounded. "Just tell us your story. Go ahead and talk."

And he did, rambling at first, telling them how hard he worked, at school, holding down two jobs. He told them how terrible life had been ever since his father had died all those years ago. But things had really veered out of control, Jason said, about six years ago, during a trip to Las Vegas, when Jane had become obsessed with singer Duncan Sheik. Jason talked about her conspiracy fears, how she'd thought people in the music industry were out to kill her. Then it was the Mexicans, then the Jews, then there were neighbors who were child molesters and after Matt.

"All just crazy, crazy stuff," Jason said. "I mean, everything was really crazy. She'd always be mad at me because I wouldn't believe it. I told her, 'You're just wacky.' So one time, I told her that, and she crushed in the side of my head with a hockey stick."

Jason told his story in a jumbled rush, emphasizing Jane's terrible temper. He wanted the detectives to understand that his mother was crazy, and he'd feared her. He'd feared her very much.

"I could tell you a million freaking stories," he said. "President Clinton hates us. President Bush hates us. Everybody hates us. They're coming to kill us. Just bullshit."

He talked about the family's period of homelessness, living out of cars and cheap motels. "It was horrible," Jason said. "I almost committed suicide so many times, you don't even know."

Once settled in Riverside, all was well for about four months, Jason acknowledged. Then, he said, Jane started again. And he got scared.

"Every day she'd freak out and say, 'They're breaking into our house,' " Jason said. "That was her big thing, people breaking in our house and putting in cameras. She'd say, 'We're on videotape for the world to see.' Yeah, my house is extremely fucking scary."

"So what eventually happened, Jason?" Andre prodded.

"She was yelling at me," he said. "I said, 'No, I don't believe that,' because I was just tired, 'and I don't want to hear it.' "

"Yeah?" said Andre, encouraging him.

"She went and got a knife," Jason said. "She said,

'Well, you don't believe me? You're going to believe me now!' And she started swinging the knife at me."

"So, she was coming at you?" he asked.

"Yeah, like coming at me," Jason affirmed. "I thought I was going to die. I got her down and I . . . I don't know, I'm a big guy. I used my strength. And, like, I . . . Well, she died."

The detectives nodded. It was the story they had been waiting to hear. But Jason was claiming self-defense. Neither detective was ready to buy that just yet.

"Jason, we need details," Andre said. "You need to be more specific."

"Well, she swung the knife at me and somehow I brought her down," he said. "And I was so freaked out, I didn't let go when I should have."

"Then what?"

"I flipped out. I mean, I cried for like half an hour."

"After, Jason," Andre asked. "What did you do to your mom after?"

"God, this is going to sound so horrible," he moaned.

"Jason, we don't hate you," Craig offered, trying to keep Jason calm.

"I wish she just would have left me alone," Jason said.

"Jason, what happened?" Andre asked.

"I just had her in a bear hug," said Jason, detailing how he had her facedown, pushing down on her neck, hard, into the carpet. "I wasn't trying to kill her. I was just trying to hold her down so she wouldn't hurt me."

"Did she scream?"

"No," Jason said. "She just said something like, 'I'm going to get you.'"

"Was she crying?"

"No, more like rage," he said.

Afterward, Jason said, he'd called out to Matt, who had been in his room throughout the struggle. Matt looked at the body, checked for a pulse. When Matt found none, Jason cried.

"I told him to get in the room, don't be in here," Jason said. "I was just thinking, I didn't think anybody knew about my mom."

"We know now," Craig said.

"I thought it was our family secret," Jason said. "I was going to call the police."

"Why didn't you?" Andre asked.

"I just didn't think people knew about my mom," Jason said. "If I thought people knew, I would've called the cops right then."

"So you thought, 'Nobody's going to notice that my mom's missing'?" asked Andre. When Jason paused, Andre pushed, "Come on, be honest."

"I mean, yeah, it wasn't like 'Nobody's going to notice she's missing,'" Jason said. "I didn't know what to do. I didn't think I could go to the police. I didn't think the police would believe me. So I started thinking, 'What can you do with the body?' Like, I'm stupid. I don't know.

"So then I was thinking about that episode I saw on *The Sopranos*," he said. "They got rid of Ralphie a certain way."

"Yeah, I saw that one," said Andre, remembering the brutal depiction of the victim losing his head and hands to prevent identification. "We need you to tell us. How did you do it?"

"Pretty much, I took off the hands, took off the head, rolled it all up in a sleeping bag, and put it in the trunk."

"Where are those items now?" Craig asked. "The head and hands?"

"Oh, the head and hands," Jason said. "I still got those. They're at my house."

"Where in the house?" Craig pushed.

"In a bag, in a closet. In a hall closet."

The detectives felt an electric jolt sweep through them. They'd been detectives a long time, but it all sounded so cold, so gruesome. Jason had lived in that apartment for over a week with his mother's head and hands tucked safely away. It was beyond gross.

"Did Matt know where they're at?"

"Yeah," Jason said. "I told him, 'Don't touch any of that shit.' I just didn't know what to do with it."

"Did he participate . . . ?" Andre began.

"He didn't participate in anything," Jason said quickly. "He didn't do a single thing."

"But he knew what you were going to do to the body?" Andre asked.

"Yeah, he knew."

"Are we going to find any information on your computer about how to kill someone, how to dismember someone, how to get rid of a body?" asked Andre, still not convinced that Jason had killed Jane on the spur of the moment, while in fear for his life.

"No, the worst thing on my computer is some porn—big deal," he said.

"How did you know where to cut?" Andre asked.

"I just picked a spot that looked good," he said.

"Was there a lot of blood?" Andre continued.

"My God," Jason said. "So much. A lot splashed in the room, in the bathroom."

"After you cut off your mom's head and hands, did you

do anything to drain off all the blood from her body?"
Andre wanted to know.

"I just pushed," Jason said. "She was facedown in the
tub and I pushed on it."

"Is the neck towards the drain?" said Andre, pushing
for every detail, even though the thought of Jason smashing down on Jane's body to drain it of fluid made him a
little sick to his stomach.

"No, the neck was toward the middle of the tub. I would
turn on the water and try to get some of the blood down
the drain."

"Are there hesitation marks on her neck?" Andre
asked.

"Yes," he said. "I was vomiting in there, so I stopped to
vomit. Most of it ended up in the toilet."

"So, you let the body hang over the tub until all the
blood kind of drained out?" said Spencer.

"Yeah."

He told them about the drive to Oceanside with Matt to
dump the body, about the confrontation with the security
guard, and of his decision, finally, to simply dump her remains off the highway.

"I was tired," Jason said. "I was going to just go home,
leave it in the trunk and decide what to do with it later.
Then, I said, 'I might as well throw it off a cliff, because
there's nothing else I can do with it.'"

Oddly, Jason took time to note what he had been wearing as he discarded what was left of Jane. As she went
over the guard rail, the body had brushed up against
Jason, leaving smears of blood all over his pants.

"Like, my favorite pair of pants," Jason said. "They
were gray. And she got all, like . . . her blood got all over
it. I mean, my favorite pair of pants, too."

The callousness of the statement shook both detectives. As he was discarding his mother, the loss of his favorite pants was more of a concern. But they didn't dwell on that now. All of that would come out in trial.

"Why was she just wearing panties?" Andre asked.

"Oh, the clothes," he said. "I thought nobody would miss her. And if we didn't leave too much evidence, like clothes . . ."

"Jason," Andre said, "what's life been like since that night?"

"It's been horrible," Jason said. "I mean, she loved us, in her own weird way. She should have just stabbed me. It would've been better than this."

Andre reached for a picture he was carrying of Jane. "Jason, I want to show you a picture of your mom."

"Please don't," he begged. "Please don't."

"Hey, man, I applaud you for being honest," said Andre, again trying to keep Jason calm. He wanted him talking as long as possible.

"But it's not going to mean shit," he said. "I'm going to jail. My life is ruined."

"Jason," said Andre, looking carefully at him. There was one more difficult question he had to ask. "Matt—is he alive?"

"Yes, Matt's alive. I love my brother."

"Then we need to talk to him," Andre said.

"For sure, for sure," Jason said.

Before detectives formally booked Jason into custody, Andre asked if he'd like to write an apology letter to his mom.

"Something from the heart," Andre told him.

"Okay," he said. "You know, I did love my mom. No matter how crazy she was, I loved my mom."

Andre pulled out a sheet of paper and left Jason alone to gather his thoughts.

Mom,

Why? I love you. It didn't have to happen. Why? You were there for me when I was a baby. Why couldn't you just be there for us now? Our life was crazy, but I know you loved us. Why? Everything could have been perfect. I almost had my degree, Matt was going to college, we finally could have been happy. I'm not mad at you. The detectives say this isn't the first time a family has had someone like you. We could have been a real family. Instead, everything was taken away. I didn't mean for you to get hurt. I love you. When I think about this it makes me want to kill myself. But I can't. I need to be there for Matt. I don't know what good I am, though. A kid with no future. Now worthless.

With love and regret,
Jason

Jason's confession over, there was only one thing left for the detectives to do. Call in his little brother.

As Andre and Craig had suspected, Matt was not at Disneyland. In fact, he was at the mall with a pal, getting fitted for tuxes. Martin Luther King High School was about to throw their Midwinter Formal, and Matt didn't plan on missing it. He already had a date—the girl who had given him the teddy bear. He couldn't wait.

Matt was just wrapping up the fitting when Jason called.

"Hey, man, I need to talk to you," he said. "Can you meet at the Jack in the Box near the apartment?"

"Sure," he said. "When?"

"Now, as soon as you can get there," Jason told him. In truth, Jason hoped that Matt had already gotten his earlier message and would never make the meeting in the parking lot of the restaurant. But even if he did, Jason fully intended to take all of the blame. Either way, Matt should be safe, he told himself. He had to be.

21

Detective Brian Sutten stood outside the small two-bedroom apartment that had belonged to the dead woman. Andre had just called with the grisly news—the torso's missing body parts were inside. Brian got word to drive to the house as soon as Andre and Craig wrapped their first interview with Jason. At that time, Jason had given away nothing. But he was nervous. Good enough reason to make a search of the house. For all they knew, more bodies were stashed away in there.

The apartment complex's manager let Brian and his team inside. They quickly ran through each room, hoping not to find more mutilated corpses. The search only took a minute. After all, the apartment was pratically bare. Aside from a cheap couch, some plastic lawn chairs, and a couple of mattresses and televisions, just nothing. Not even a refrigerator. Thankfully, they found no more victims. Shortly after, Andre called back.

"Check the hall closet," he told Brian. "That's where he says they are."

Brian grimaced. He wasn't looking forward to that discovery. It took a while for a full search warrant to arrive. Only then could he lead his team back inside. Brian and Forensic Specialist Kevin Andera walked toward the hall closet and swung back the door. There, nestled between the coats and a pair of dress shoes, was a black duffel bag.

"That's got to be it," Brian said.

After firing off a few photos to document the discovery, Kevin reached in and pulled out the bag. He unzipped the top and pulled apart the straps to reveal bunched-up brown plastic bags, like the kind you get at the supermarket to carry groceries home. If the remains were in there, they weren't visible yet. More odd, there was no odor. Human tissue decomposing for over a week should give off a pretty horrific smell, Kevin noted.

"Well, maybe this isn't it," Brian wondered aloud.

Kevin reached inside and pulled out the bags. Nothing inside. He pulled more out, still empty. But underneath, he found a black trash bag, twisted at the top. The detectives and officers scouring the scene pulled in closer as Kevin untangled the bag to reveal its contents—a pair of hands and a face partially covered by long strands of red hair.

The small collection of left-over body parts looked more like some bizarre exhibit in a wax museum. "It doesn't even look real," said Brian. "It's not even decomposed."

Kevin nodded in agreement. The whole time, he'd had an air-purifying respirator sitting next to him, ready to absorb the foul odor that the decaying remains would undoubtedly give off. But even the stench was missing.

"Well, he's got everything wrapped up here in so many bags," Kevin said. "I guess it preserved everything. It wasn't exposed to any air."

As Kevin snapped more photos, Brian pulled himself away from the surreal scene. He walked toward the kitchen, where investigators discovered a box of cheap, unused kitchen knives. The butcher knife and scissors were missing from the set. They were set apart, in an empty kitchen drawer.

In the bathroom, another investigator covered the walls, floor, sink, and tub in Luco Crystal Violet—a chemical that reacts with even the smallest droplets of blood to turn purple. Despite Jason's diligent scrubbing with bleach, small violet spots still lit up the bathroom. It was the same story in the living room, underneath the white throw rug Jason had bought to cover the blood spatters that had spilled from his mother during their struggle.

With this much evidence, Brian thought, Jason and Matthew would certainly be charged with first-degree murder. If they ever saw the light of day again, they would be very lucky indeed.

It was early evening by the time Matt pulled into the fast food restaurant's parking lot to meet his brother. He was only 15, too young to qualify for a California driver's license, but he was behind the wheel of that ratty Honda Accord Wagon anyway. Now that Jason had sole access to the Oldsmobile, he had given Matthew permission to drive, Jane no longer being there to cart him around.

"That's him," Jason told detectives as he sat in the back of an unmarked police cruiser. "In the Honda, that's Matt."

Matt parked and began walking toward Jason, but he didn't get very far. A pair of investigators greeted him instead. Matt said nothing as they identified themselves. Wordlessly, the young suspect followed them to their car so he could be driven to the Orange County Sheriff's Department. If he'd gotten Jason's earlier warning message, he never mentioned it. But he certainly didn't need to ask what was happening. He knew.

"Now what?" Jason asked investigators as they made the drive back to sheriff's headquarters. "What happens now? Because Matt had nothing to do with this. I did everything. I just don't want him running from you guys. This was all me."

Investigators didn't know whether to believe Jason just yet. But it didn't matter, anyway. According to California law, it didn't matter which one had reached out to strangle Jane. It didn't matter who'd wielded the knife to do the slicing. If Matt had helped with the planning and cover-up, he was just as responsible.

Back at the station, Matt spun his own set of lies for Craig and Andre.

"My mom's in Belize," he told them. "That's where her boyfriend lives. I've never met him. It's just some guy she met off the Internet."

This time, the investigators were less tolerant of the tall tales. They knew too much now, so they could jump right to the point.

"Matt, Jason already told us everything, so there's no point in lying," Andre said. "What we need from you is the truth."

Confronted with his brother's confession, Matt gave up. There was no use in trying to cover up for a brother who'd already divulged so much. So he told them, "Yes, he killed her. But I wasn't there when it happened."

The detectives didn't believe Matt, and told him they thought the two had planned her death together.

Matt acknowledged that Jane's behavior had bothered them and that sometimes they'd joke that "she'd have to die or something." But he never meant it. "I'm not a killer," he said.

Matt recounted how the last fight had broken out. He

was so tired of listening to the constant bickering that he'd left, intent on taking a walk until everyone calmed down.

"I came home about thirty minutes later and Jason just told me to go to her room and not come out until he said it was okay," Matt said. "So I did."

On the way, Matt said, he'd noticed the blood spots on the floor, but he didn't ask questions. As Matt watched TV in Jane's room much later, Jason had come to him, looking disheveled, and ordered him to "help dump something," he said.

"And you never asked what that something was?"

"No, I never asked."

Both detectives were still suspicious of Matt's story. First, it differed from Jason's version. Second, it's hard to believe he'd see the blood and not even ask what had happened to his mom. He wasn't even curious where Jane was.

Matt said he'd suspected it was his mother's body getting dumped that night. But it wasn't until the next day that Jason finally told him Jane was dead. And Matt claimed he didn't call the police out of fear.

"I didn't know if what happened to her would happen to me," Matt said. "I didn't think he'd kill her, but he did. What's to stop him from killing me?"

"So you were too scared to call the police?" Andre asked.

"Yeah, I was," said Matt.

It was hard to get much out of Matt. He spoke in two-to three-word sentences. But mostly, it was odd to watch the teenager talk so coldly about his mom's slaying. He never cried, never got upset, spoke mostly in a monotone.

He could have been talking about last night's homework assignment for all the emotion he showed, Andre thought.

"Did you know her head and hands were in the closet?" Andre asked.

"Yeah, I knew."

"Didn't that bother you?"

"No, I just blocked it out."

"But you had friends over, right? What did you tell them?"

"I just told them to stay out of the closet," Matt said.

Again, the investigators were shocked by the callousness of his answers. With that kind of coldness, it was clear—maybe he hadn't physically laid his hands on Jane and strangled her to death, as Jason had, but he didn't mind that the job had been done.

"Did she ever hurt you, Matt?" Andre asked.

"Yeah, she hit me a couple of times, but Jason took most of it," Matt said. "It's because she hated his dad."

"Are you sad she's gone?" Andre asked.

"Yeah, I am," he said, before adding, "I loved her. But she deserved it."

The detectives had one more idea before booking the boys. They led Matt into an empty room and sat him there, alone, for several minutes. Then, in walked Jason. The brothers looked at each other in surprise. Jason caught on immediately. He quickly walked over to his little brother and dipped low, whispering into his ear.

The detectives looking on from behind a mirrored window had to give the boy credit. "He knows we're taping them," Andre said. "I'm sure he just told Matthew as much."

There was an awkward pause before Jason broke the silence.

"Hey, man, I love you," he told Matt. "And I'm going to take all of this."

"I'm going to go to jail, Jason," Matt said flatly. "I can't believe I'm going to jail."

"No, you're not," Jason shot back. "I told the detectives you did nothing. They believe me. They know Mom is crazy. They know she came at me with a knife."

Andre couldn't help but get the feeling that Jason was carefully choosing his words for the audiotape.

"I'll probably die in prison, man," Jason said. "But I told them how Mom came at me with that knife."

"Dude, our lives are ruined," Matt said.

"No," Jason answered. "Not your life. Just mine."

They hugged for a moment. Then big brother offered more advice.

"Listen, when you're in there, in juvenile hall, you take care of yourself," Jason said. "You can't be a punk. And don't tell them what you're in here for. Got it?"

Matthew nodded, soaking up Jason's words. At that moment, he had never loved, and hated, his brother more.

"I just don't believe it," Andre told Craig as they stood outside the interview room. "I don't believe this whole self-defense story or that Matt was gone and knew nothing about what was happening, what he was dumping. They both knew this was going to happen and the whole thing was planned out. That's what I think."

Then he sighed. Despite the confession, despite the body and the discovery of the murder weapon, he still had a lot of work to do.

Nearly twenty-five minutes passed before the detectives put an end to the reunion. Jason, then Matthew, stood for mug shots. Then both were photographed again, naked, for evidence purposes. All was quiet as Matthew rode to Orange County Juvenile Hall, Jason to Santa Ana Jail, both held on suspicion of violating penal code 187—homicide.

It was the morning of January 27, 2003, when Orange County Sheriff Michael S. Carona organized a press conference announcing the arrest. For a top cop, there are few prouder moments than announcing an arrest in a blockbuster case. The headless torso discovery had been broadcast all over the news for days. Now, the sheriff was not only announcing the body's identity, but he could also tell the small army of print, television, and radio reporters that his investigators had done their job. The murderers, Jane's 15- and 20-year-old sons, were in custody, held in lieu of $1 million bail. After a lot of good old-fashioned detective work, the boys had been arrested and interviewed, and had ultimately confessed.

"Jason told investigators he and his brother were involved in the killing and dismemberment of their mother," Sheriff Carona announced.

Shocked reporters clamored for more. They wanted details. They wanted a motive.

"I don't know what motive you could possibly give for killing your mother, cutting off her head, and cutting off her hands," answered Carona simply.

Sons collaborating to kill Mom—that alone made for a sensational story. Matricide cases didn't happen very often. But the real selling point, as far as reporters were concerned, came next.

"Jason told investigators he had seen an episode of *The Sopranos*," Sheriff Carona explained, "and that's where he saw the same type of dismemberment done before dumping a body."

The story made instant headlines: " 'Sopranos' Scenario in Slaying?" declared the *Los Angeles Times*. "Sheriff: Sons say they dismembered mom after watching 'The Sopranos,'" read an Associated Press story. " 'Sopranos' called sons' inspiration," proclaimed Riverside County's *Press-Enterprise*. Even the National Italian American Foundation issued a press release that claimed, "By promoting violence and worshipping at the altar of *gangsterism*, 'The Sopranos' has produced an ugly scene. The time has long passed for HBO to put the public interest before concern for profit. The blood of Jane Bautista's family in Orange County, California is on their hands. The public has a right to know what HBO is going to do about it."

Reporters flooded HBO studios for a comment. But the cable network's executives had little to say. The highly rated show had already come under considerable fire for its use of excessive violence in story lines. This kind of publicity was the last thing they needed.

Meanwhile, those who'd known Jane and the boys over the years were shocked at the news.

Stacie Eldrige stood dressing for morning classes in front of the television when she caught the news report announcing an arrest in connection with the headless corpse found off the Ortega Highway. Jason Bautista, the report said, was the main suspect in the slaying of his mother, along with little brother Matthew Montejo. Stacie paused.

"What?" she said to no one in particular. "I know a Jason Bautista, but it just can't be the same one." She scrambled out of the house to pick up a morning paper. And there it was, his picture on the front page. It looked just like Jason, but without glasses. Stacie picked up a black ink pen and drew a pair around the eyes. That was him, her gut knew it. Still, she didn't want to believe it, not even when the accompanying story gave the details: a biochemistry major at California State University, a Riverside resident. Instead, she ran toward the school's lunch room, where she routinely met him for coffee.

"I was still hoping to see him sitting there, like I always do, flipping through the newspaper," Stacie recalled. "But he wasn't there. That's when I knew for sure."

Sarah Reinelt got a call from a classmate instructing her to go find the nearest newspaper. She ran downstairs to find her father casually reading over the morning's headlines.

"Dad," she said breathlessly, "my friend just called and said my lab partner is on the front page of the paper for murdering his mom." Her dad simply set the paper down and pointed to the story he was reading, complete with a picture of Jason.

Talk spread like wildfire across the campus, especially in the small computer lab where investigators ripped out and confiscated Jason's personal locker for evidence. The science department invited counselors over to discuss the arrest with shocked students and even a few stunned members of the faculty. Some cried at the waste of it all, knowing Jason would likely never fulfill all the dreams he so fervently talked about.

"At first, we all just wanted to defend him," Stacie said. "Because it's just so hard to believe. That is not the Jason that we knew at all."

Dan Huffer, the general manager at the hotel where Jason worked, saw the same news reports and was shocked into silence. He knew the police had been looking for Jason since they'd come to the hotel days before. But he never would have guessed this was the reason. He shook his head and instantly thought back to a call he'd gotten. Jason had phoned on what was, Huffer now realized, the day of his arrest, to say he wouldn't be in to work for a few days. Family emergency, he'd said. Jason had been calling from the police station, though Dan didn't know that at the time.

"Unbelievable," Huffer said as he made the connection. "Here's this kid in a crapload of trouble, and his first call is to me saying he's not coming to work."

Interestingly, Matt's old soccer coach and team mom, Brad and Nancy Joplin, had a very different reaction to the news. They'd heard Jane's frantic tales so many times, stories of running from bad men out to kill her, that they couldn't help but think about it now.

"I'll tell you how believable she was with her stories," Brad said. "When we found out what happened, our first thought was, 'Oh God, she was telling the truth all along. They finally got her. And the kids are being framed for it.'"

Also watching the news reports that day was Jose Montejo's brother, who lived in California. He recognized the names from so many years ago—Jane Bautista, her son Jason Bautista, son Matthew Montejo. He called Jose.

"Hey," he said, "have you seen the news? The police arrested your son Matt because he killed Jane."

Jose dropped the phone and ran to flip on the television. Channel 9 was running the report, complete with Jason's booking mug shot flashing across the screen. He sank to his knees and began to cry. "What the hell happened?" he said to himself. Then he remembered how

much Jane had hated Jason. And he knew that if Jason did
kill her, he'd had reason. Jose got on the phone and called
the sheriff's department. He wanted them to know Matt
couldn't have been involved. Jane had loved Matthew,
just as much as she'd hated Jason.

22

It fell to Andre and Craig to begin follow-up interviews with members of Jane's family in Illinois. They may not have spoken to their daughter in years, but they had to be told the news. And they might be able to shed some light on Jason's story.

Jane's frail grandmother took the call from the coroner's office. She was still recovering from a major heart attack and felt weak as a bird. Now this news. It was almost more than she could stand. Jane, her beloved granddaughter, the one who used to clean her house for pocket money years ago, the one she still sent checks to every month, had been murdered? Charlie Mae was devastated.

"That news really got the best of me," she would say later.

Charlie Mae immediately called next door to her daughter, Nellie, Jane's mom. Nellie immediately called her brother, Jim Funderburk, who was coincidentally driving through California by motor home on his way back from a Mexican vacation with his wife. Since their father's retirement, and now death, Jim had been the real patriarch of the family, anyway. He had been running the business for years and took to calling most of the shots for the Funderburk clan. He agreed to drive into Orange County and told Nellie and her husband to get on a plane as soon as possible.

The meeting between Craig and Andre and the family

at sheriff's headquarters was cordial enough, the investigators recall. The family confirmed some of what the boys had said—Jane was mentally ill—and made it clear that they were there to support the boys. Jim asked to see Matthew in juvenile hall.

That's when all signs of cordiality faded.

"We can't do that," Andre said. "It's not visiting hours right now."

Jim could care less about visiting hours. He wanted to see Matthew or Jason right now.

"You guys could make this happen if you wanted to," he shot at them.

"No, we can't," Craig confirmed. "That's not up to us."

"Then we have nothing more to say," Jim told them before directing his family out the door.

Afterward, Andre and Craig thought it very odd that during the entire conversation, they'd had very few questions about Jane.

"In fact, they never asked about Jane's death at all," Craig said.

During normal visiting hours, the boys' extended family stopped by to see them. Because of their high-profile case, Matthew and Jason had become protective custody prisoners, meaning interaction with other inmates would be strictly limited. Fellow prisoners have a tendency to go after those with too much notoriety. On top of that, even criminals have a code of conduct. Those who commit crimes considered especially horrific, like the molestation of a child, are targets for attack behind bars. Slicing off your mother's head would certainly fall into that category.

Their protective custody status, however, didn't prevent them from seeing outside visitors. Relatives saw Jason first, since he was the easiest to gain access to. Matthew, held in juvenile hall, required a court order for access. On January 28, 2003, Judge Ronald Kueber granted visiting rights to Jim Funderburk, Nellie Osborne, Deborah Cagle (Jane's sister), and Rita Holland (Deborah's 23-year-old daughter). Only now that Jane was dead, and her sons in custody for her murder, did the family rally around the boys. It's hard to say whether anyone felt guilty for not doing more to intervene, like raising the boys in a safe home while Jane went into a hospital. But now, the boys learned that their relatives didn't blame them for what had happened. The family would support them in any way possible—including letters, phone calls, the occasional visit, and, most important, money for a decent defense attorney.

That same day, the boys were scheduled to make their first court appearance. Case jurisdiction was still being decided, but the prosecutor was pretty sure he'd stay with it. "We've put so much work into this one," he told his bosses, "we can't let it go now. The investigation will lose momentum and the entire case will suffer." Ultimately, even the other side agreed, and Mike Murray got what he wanted—the okay to try the case.

In court, Mike first laid eyes on the boys accused of doing the unthinkable. So many questions still hung in his mind: Why did they do it? Was there insurance money? Was there abuse? And if so, why didn't the older son just move out? Or at least report the abuse?

Both boys entered not guilty pleas to the murder charges, their defense attorneys, paid with Funderburk money, at their sides.

Outside court, Matthew's attorney raged about his juvenile client entering a plea in adult court alongside his adult brother. "He belongs in juvenile court where his

name is not being published all over the world," defense
attorney Stephen Klarich told the group of reporters covering the story. He also demanded a hearing as soon as
possible to seek Matthew's immediate release. "My client
was not involved in any crime."

Jason's attorney had his own spin for the press. "This is
a homicide that may very well have been justified," John
M. Kremer told reporters. "Something was very, very
wrong in that household. Clearly, something triggered all
of this."

Mike Murray was having a hard time watching the
show. Jane may have been delusional, but it was difficult
to believe she could have done anything to deserve such a
brutal end. By all accounts, she was mentally unstable.
But she was sick, not evil. "And as nutty as she may have
been," Mike would say after the court appearance, "her
life was those two boys—feeding them, clothing them,
getting them to and from school. This was not a woman
who got money from family and spent it on weekends at
the spa, who left her kids hungry, or didn't value their education. You can say a lot of things about Jane, but she
made sure her kids got what they needed. Even through
her deepest delusions, she made sure of that."

For that reason, Mike made the call—15-year-old
Matthew would stand trial as an adult. Tried as a juvenile,
he'd be out by his twenty-fifth birthday. Mike couldn't see
a 10-year sentence for a boy who, at minimum, sat by
while his mother was brutally murdered. He'd committed
an adult crime, and would pay the price like an adult.

After court, Jason sat in a sheriff's department van
surrounded by fellow inmates who'd also made court
appearances that morning. During the ride back to jail,

Jason struck up a conversation with April Valenzuela, a petite young single mom who had landed in jail, arrested for a series of misdemeanor violations, including bouncing checks, burglary, and theft. If not for her jail suit and cuffs, the raven-haired girl would have looked like a teenager who should be shuffling off to her next class. She told Jason her offenses and expected to hear a similar story from the young, well-mannered, articulate boy sitting next to her. Instead, she was stunned into silence.

"I'm here because I killed my mother," he told her, grinning wide as he said it.

"Really?" was all April could think to say. She had a hard time believing it.

"Really," he answered. "I'm Bautista. Jason Bautista. I'm the one on the cover of *People* magazine last week!" The detail about the cover was a lie, but the magazine had written about the slaying.

April just stared in disbelief—not only had he apparently killed his mom, he was bragging about it, even boasting of a magazine cover story like he was some superstar. A chill ran through her. If true, this guy was too creepy.

23

Andre and Craig had a lot of interviews ahead of them. They wanted to talk to as many people as possible to figure out how much of Jason's story was true, and how much was made up by a scared and desperate young man to get out of trouble. They believed Jane had been mentally ill—but that didn't justify killing her. They needed to know if Jane had really gone after her son with a knife that night. Or had Jason planned the entire murder because it was easier to get rid of Mom than move out, leave his great-grandmother's monthly $1,500 stipends behind, and start over on his own?

Since family members were hostile toward them, the investigators decided to start chatting with friends of the boys.

Casey Kritzer said she hadn't known Jason very long. Just a few months, since she'd started working at the Hilton. She liked him a lot, she said, even though not everyone at the hotel did—including manager Crystal Cantu, who thought he was a smartass. Casey said he was always kind to her. They'd hung out after work a few times, she told them. But just as friends. "I'm married," she emphasized.

"Did Jason talk much about his mom?" Andre asked.

"Not too much," she said.

"When did he last mention her?"

"In December," she said. "He told me she was moving to Chicago."

The detectives paused at the news. December? That was a month before Jane died. Could it be true that Jane really had been planning on going home to be with the relatives she'd supposedly hated and hadn't talked to in years? Or had Jason been laying the groundwork to explain her upcoming disappearance?

"Chicago," Andre repeated. "Interesting. Did he say why she was moving?"

"She had a sick grandmother back there, I guess, and she was going to go home to take care of her," Casey told them. "He said she'd be leaving for good in a couple of weeks."

"Was Jason supposed to go with her?" Andre asked.

"No, he was going to stay for school, and so was his little brother," Casey said. "He said he'd just end up taking care of Matt so he wouldn't have to change schools or anything. Plus, Jason said he already paid a lot of the rent and bills, so he didn't think it was going to be a problem making it on his own."

Especially since he'd continue to cash Grandma Mae's checks, Andre thought. Detectives had already discovered that her last check had been cashed, even though it was sent after Jane's death.

Later, detectives tracked down Sarah Reinelt, who described herself as a very good friend of Jason's. She was still stunned by the news. There had to be something more to the story, she told them. Jason, the one she knew, was much too gentle to kill anyone.

"Well, we're trying to find out the truth," Andre said. "That's why we're here."

She knew Jason hadn't always gotten along with his

mother. But the situation didn't seem serious. He rarely even spoke about it. But he did seem pretty chipper when she decided to move back to Chicago, Sarah recalled.

"What did he say about that, exactly?" Andre pressed.

"Just that she was going back indefinitely to take care of a sick grandmother," Sarah said. "He was pretty excited to get his car back, too."

"His car back? The Honda?"

"No, the Intrigue. He said it was really his, because he made the payments on it, but that his mom just borrowed it all the time. He was really happy about that. He used to call the other car 'the ratty station wagon.' He hated that car."

Sarah said she'd really only run into Jason one other time that month, in the computer lab. He was sitting quietly in front of a terminal watching what looked like a movie, she said.

"*The Sopranos*," he'd told her. "It's my favorite show."

January 13 would be Jane's last day of life. But that afternoon, Jason had seemed like a guy without a care in the world, remembered Jason's classmate William Shadrick. Shadrick was a Cal State graduate already. But he hoped to go to graduate school, so he'd returned to campus that afternoon to order some transcripts and had run into his old friend lunching in the computer lab.

"Jason told me if I was going to be in town awhile that I should come over to his place sometime," William told the detectives. "It shocked me, because he never really got along very well with his mother." Once, while talking about an argument with her, Jason lashed out, "I'll kill that bitch one day," William recalled. But he hadn't given the statement much weight. "I just got the feeling it was something he just said. I didn't think he meant it. I didn't take it seriously."

"Had he ever invited you over before?"

"No, never," William said. "I asked, you know, 'What about your mom?' And he just said, 'She won't care because she moved to Chicago to live with her sick grandmother.'"

"He told you she had already moved?" Andre asked.

"Yeah," William answered.

Jason hadn't talked about Jane much, William said. But the few times he had, it was obvious how much he'd hated her. William remembered his friend's voice whenever he spoke of her: "He said she was a bitch. He was very angry about it. There was always just this kind of rage."

Finally, Andre and Craig caught up with Jason's lab partner, Stephen Kavousy. He told them all about the cryptic song lyric Jason had sung in early January: "It always amazes me how I can kill a man and it doesn't faze me."

Craig and Andre found the lyric a stunning piece of evidence and set out to track down the song. Ultimately, they never found an exact match to the line. Interestingly, however, there's a song eerily similar to the one Stephen remembered his pal singing. The lyric, by the band No Crash, actually reads, "Death, it doesn't phase [sic] me. But people crying over dying never ceases to amaze me." The tune is called "Kill Your Parents."

But even as Stephen remembered it, the detectives considered Jason's lyric strong proof that he had been thinking about murder. He had known he was going to kill his mom, known it for weeks, at least. But to cover their bases, they needed to talk to Grandma Mae. Certainly, if her favorite granddaughter had been planning a move

home, she would have known about it. It was time to visit
Winthrop Harbor.

Getting an interview with Charlie Mae Funderburk was
going to be tough. So far, Jane's parents and uncle refused
to help with the murder investigation. Craig Johnson decided not to call first. He'd just hop a plane out, this time
bringing Investigator Dennis Burke with him for help,
and try the element of surprise.

The Funderburk relatives were "big fishes in a small
pond," as Craig put it. Since he was going to be on their
turf, there could be trouble. He contacted Winthrop Harbor
Police Detective Sergeant Tim Borowski for extra insurance. Tim knew the family well. They were very influential
in the community because of their well-known construction company and resulting wealth. But they were also
deeply private people. The detectives would certainly have
a hard time getting cooperation, he acknowledged.

"The family, especially Jim, wants to keep this very
private," Tim said. "They don't want anyone talking about
it." In short, they apparently found the murder an embarrassing, private family tragedy that needed to be forgotten
as soon as possible. But Tim also knew the interviews had
to be conducted.

"Come on down and I'll help you in any way I can," he
said.

Shortly after arriving in Winthrop, Dennis and Craig
met up with Tim in front of Charlie Mae Funderburk's
house. If she was alone, they reasoned, she just might
talk. And that conversation could be very enlightening,
given she was the only relative aside from the boys whom
Jane had ever trusted.

In truth, Jane talked to Grandma Mae frequently

following August 30, 2002, when her grandfather, the patriarch of the family and the man responsible for the Funderburk clan's financial success, had died at the age of 86. His heart had simply given out, despite the insertion of a pacemaker just days before. His passing devastated Jane's beloved grandmother. The couple had been married sixty-eight years. Now, she felt alone. In sporadic phone calls, Mae had begged her granddaughter to come home. But for some reason, Jane never returned, not even for the funeral.

"Jim's probably going to get mad if we don't let him know first," Tim said.

"I know," Craig told him. "But I don't care. I don't need him standing in my way."

They knocked on her door. She was alone—a small miracle, since she still lived next door to her daughter and son-in-law. But clearly, Charlie Mae was hungry for attention. Like a lot of elderly widows, she longed for someone to talk to. Likely she didn't get a lot of visitors. And her own failing health kept her homebound. So she eagerly sat with the kind detectives, telling them anything they wanted to know.

"Are you from California?" Charlie Mae wanted to know.

"Yes, we flew all the way out here just to talk to you," Craig told her.

"Well, now . . . Now, you'll have to talk kind of loud," Charlie Mae told them. "I'm kind of hard of hearing."

"I'm here regarding your granddaughter," Craig began. "You heard what happened? About her being murdered?"

"Pardon?"

"You heard about your granddaughter?" he tried again, louder.

"Yes!"

"And she was murdered."

"Pardon?"

This was going to take a while, Craig sighed to himself. He breathed in deeply and tried again, very loudly. "You heard she was murdered?"

"I heard that."

"And the two boys are in custody," Craig said.

"She had two boys?" she asked, as if hearing the news for the first time.

"Yes, Jason and Matthew," Craig said. "Basically, what I'm trying to clear up is, was Jane planning to come back here and take care of you?"

"Oh yes, yes she was," Charlie Mae said, explaining how Jane had talked about coming home even before her Grandpa Ben had died. "She said, 'Me and Matt will stay with you and I'll take care of you and Grandpa.' But then my husband died two or three months later."

Jane had skipped the funeral, saying her asthma was acting up too badly. But she'd promised to come home for Christmas, Charlie Mae said. "Then she called again before Thanksgiving and said, 'We can't come for December. We can't afford it right now.'"

"But she never had a definite plan to come back?" Craig asked, desperate for some clarification. It sounded to him like the idea of coming home was something Jane had just said to appease her ailing grandmother, not something she'd actually meant.

"I don't know, she just kept saying, 'Grandma, I'm coming back to take care of you and Grandpa.' Her and I were very, very close."

"What do you think about this whole thing?" Craig asked.

"I just can't believe it," she said. "But I know it must be true. Did you interview them?"

"Yes," he told her. "Jason told me what happened."

"Well, I'm shocked that he'd do that, as much as his mother thought of him. Oh, she worked so hard to raise them kids. Once she got so upset and she called me saying she didn't know what to do about them. And I said, 'I'll send money every month, don't you worry.'"

Craig nodded, thinking about the $1,000 to $2,000 checks dropped into Jane's post office box every month, like clockwork, for all those years.

"To this day I don't know exactly what happened," Charlie Mae continued. "I've been in the hospital twice now. Jim gave the doctors orders to tell me nothing. Jim just told me that they picked up the boys and they are in jail and everybody was nice to him . . . You know, I've just had a bad time."

Craig could see that. So he wasn't going to take the time now to fill her in on the gruesome details surrounding her favorite granddaughter's death. Instead, he listened to her talk about watching Nellie feed her dying father applesauce at the hospital; about Funderburk houses and how they were more expensive, but worth it; about her own trips—two of them—to the hospital since her husband's death; about her other granddaughter, Jane's sister, who lived in Texas but owned property in Winthrop. He listened for twenty minutes, letting her talk like she probably hadn't talked in years, before finally extending his business card and breaking the news that they had to go.

"But I just want to make sure one more time. Jane never set a date to come out here, right? There was no plane ticket or anything?"

"No, there was no date set, no ticket," Charlie Mae repeated.

"Because you were going to send her a ticket if she really wanted to come?"

"Yes," Charlie Mae said. "Don't think I wouldn't. I would."

That was all they needed. The investigators now believed for certain that Jane had never had any real intentions to move. And Jason knew it. It was just his convenient cover.

"Do you know what Jane said to me the last time I talked to her just before Thanksgiving?" Charlie Mae asked. "She said, 'Grandma, do you know what a hard time I had raising them boys? Will you pray for me that I live to get my kids grown?' She said those very words to me."

Craig and Dennis didn't know what to say. They were remarkably prophetic words.

"Are you going to call Jim while you're here?"

"Yes," Craig told her.

"Oh, that's good," she said. "I think he'll like you."

Craig could only smile, knowing that nothing was farther from the truth.

Tim thought for sure they'd find Jim at the family's restaurant, the Stone Creek Grill. Sure enough, he was there, sitting at a table and sipping on a beer.

"Hey, Mr. Funderburk," Craig said. "Remember me?"

"Yes," he said, cordially enough, and nodding a greeting to Tim. If he was surprised to see the detective, he showed no sign of it.

"We need to talk to you for a minute," Craig told him.

"Okay, let's go on outside," he answered, rising to lead

them out the front door, away from eavesdropping ears.

"Listen," Craig said, once outside. "We're here to talk to Charlie Mae."

"Well, she's not feeling too well today," he said. "I'll call you when she's better."

Exactly what the detective had expected to hear.

"No," Craig said. "You don't understand. We already talked to her. I just wanted to let you know."

Jim bristled, gripping his beer bottle tightly. "I really wish you hadn't done that," he said. "I don't think that's right, and you shouldn't have done that."

"Hey," Craig reminded him. "We're just trying to find the truth. And we need to talk to anyone who can help us get there. We can sit and talk to anyone, anywhere, anytime that wants to help."

"No," Jim said. "I don't think anyone else has anything more to say to you."

"Don't you want the truth to come out, Jim?" asked Craig, hoping Jim would find some sympathy for his slain mentally disturbed niece. Clearly she'd lived a hard life. Clearly she had been sick. But the family had never even tried to get her help. They'd just ignored her throughout her life. Now, in death, they would do the same.

"I don't think the family has anything to say to you," he said again. And that was the end of the conversation.

As he retreated, Craig made a mental note to thank Tim for coming. With a temper like that, who knows how that interaction would have escalated if not for the local cop's presence?

24

In the weeks since the murder, Jose Montejo had longed to renew his relationship with Matthew. Jose was still living in San Diego County, less than an hour's drive from the Santa Ana Jail and juvenile hall. So, by the end of January, just days after Matt's arrest, Jose stopped by the jail to pay his long-lost son a visit. He barely recognized the boy who came through the metal doors to sit before him. He didn't know why, but he'd expected to see Matt bounding out of the gate still looking like the small boy he'd left behind so many years ago. Jose barely recognized the tall, skinny 15-year-old kid looking at him.

"Do you hate me, Dad?" Matt asked him.

"No, no, Matt," Jose told him. "I could never hate you. I love you, no matter what."

"Why didn't you come find me?" Matt asked. "You know what she was like."

"I looked for you for a long time," Jose said. "But your mom, I thought she had a restraining order. And then I couldn't find you. But I'm here now."

That may have sounded like an excuse to a lot of kids. But Matt didn't have many people in his corner just then. The support of a long-absent dad was better than no dad at all. Unbeknownst to Jose, it was actually one of Matt's defense attorneys, David Cohn, who'd encouraged Matt to open up to his dad.

"I know he's my dad," Matt had told David. "But I hate him for leaving us all these years."

"Just listen to what he has to say," David had told him. "You have plenty of catching up to do."

Now Jose was the most consistent visitor Matt had. Jose had remarried over the last decade and had two little girls, Matt's half-sisters. "They're your family now, too," Jose told him.

Jose wanted to see Jason, too, offering his support to the young man he still considered his "other son." But Jason refused to see Jose. He hadn't wanted to talk to anyone outside of his uncle and grandmother in the first few weeks after his arrest. But when Jim and Nellie returned to their lives in Winthrop Harbor, Jason had nobody. No one came to see him for weeks, and he grew lonely. Finally, he sent a letter to Matt telling him it would be okay if Jose wanted to stop by sometime. So he did, coming in to see Jason after an afternoon visit with Matt. It was an awkward meeting at first, Jose recalled. Jason looked stoic behind the glass and said little. Jose couldn't help thinking that Jason had grown up to be a lot like the mother he had just killed.

"That's the amazing thing," Jose would say later of that first meeting. "I kept thinking, his mother treated him so bad, but he's just like her. He's very smart, but secretive and hard to get to know, just like Jane."

At the preliminary hearing on June 6, 2003, Matt's attorney had one goal—getting Matt home. A preliminary hearing was the prosecution's chance to lay out all the evidence gathered against a defendant, thus convincing a judge there was enough to bring the case to trial. It was the rare hearing indeed when a judge ruled against a prosecutor. Especially in a murder case. Generally, the prosecutor got the benefit of the doubt, and the case progressed effortlessly to trial.

David thought maybe this time a judge could see that Matt had had nothing to do with Jane's death. It would be a tough fight, though. David was up against one of the most aggressive prosecutors in the district attorney's office. Mike Murray had never lost a case. David, meanwhile, had assisted on several murder cases, but he'd never taken one in front of a jury.

Nellie and Jim flew out for the hearing. A few of Jason's friends from the Chemistry Club showed up, too, including his pal Stacie. Reporters filled the courtroom.

Jason and Matt were seated together. It was the first time they'd seen each other since the arrest in January, and they chatted animatedly before things got under way. About nothing, mostly—the Lakers, music, what jail life was like. Matt was going to school behind bars. Ironically, his grades were better than ever. "I've never had this much structure," he once told David. "My structure at home was yelling." But there were a few scuffles with fellow inmates, mostly those who took to calling Matt "Mommy Killer."

Andre Spencer was the star witness of the day. He recounted Jason's confession and Matt's story about dumping the body. Andre also testified about a conversation he'd had with one of Matt's fellow inmates, who'd asked Matt what he was in for.

"Because of the woman found off the Ortega Highway," Matt had told her. "They don't even know everything about why we did it."

Then it was up to the attorneys to argue their positions.

Jason's attorney, John Kremer, called the slaying a spur-of-the-moment tragedy rising from Jason's desperate struggle to defend himself. But it was doubtful he'd go home today. The evidence against him, including his own confession, was too overwhelming.

Then David spoke, zeroing in on the lack of evidence linking Matt to the murder.

"He was a fifteen-year-old boy who hated his mother on occasion. Maybe she didn't let him go where he wanted and do what he wanted. But there's no evidence he wanted her dead. And once he found out his brother killed her, he thought maybe, since his brother did this to her, he could do that to him, too. He's in circumstances a fifteen-year-old should never be in. And what does a fifteen-year-old child do when caught in this kind of circumstance? The best he can. He listens to his brother."

But Mike mocked the idea that Matt was some scared little boy, too frightened to call for help.

"He's on top of the world," Mike told the judge. "He's driving the family car, making plans to go to the Winter Formal. He's got friends over to hang out, all while his mom's head and hands are in a bag on a shelf in the hallway closet! This is a boy who is quite capable of lying, quite capable of covering up facts, and quite capable of carrying on with life as usual."

Judge John D. Conley barely paused a moment before making his ruling.

"I find many elements of this story hard to believe," he said. "Jason says, 'Go to your room,' 'Go watch TV,' 'Come out to the car with me,' 'Help me to the Dumpster,' and Matt just goes along and never asks a question?"

Matt looked at the floor as the judge spoke, his chances of walking away today rapidly dwindling.

"Just think what happened to this poor woman," Conley

continued. "How she was carved up, and Matt knew nothing about it because he was sitting around watching TV?"

He ordered Jason to stand trial, though that was never really in question. Then he turned to Matt and ordered him on to trial, too.

After court, Stacie introduced herself to Nellie and Jim, letting them know how much she'd liked Jason when they went to school together. Stacie couldn't help but wonder if the family had known Jane was sick.

"Yes," Nellie said. "We knew Jane had mental illness issues. We guessed it was hard for those kids. But what could we do? You don't just step in and take someone else's kids. It wasn't our business."

Stacie was stunned. Jane's mom was saying her child's mental illness and her grandchildren's well-being were none of her business? "But that was her attitude," Stacie said later. "Just kind of neither here nor there. But they knew there was a problem. Everyone in the family knew it. It was no secret."

As the preliminary hearing wrapped, Mike decided to add another charge. Since the boys had told friends before the murder happened that Jane was planning a move to Chicago, clearly they had discussed the murder in advance. That was conspiracy, a charge that by itself carries a 25-year sentence.

Bringing any felony case to trial can be expensive. But a murder trial? Not only are there countless billable hours from the attorney, but investigation costs to cover trips to interview witnesses. Fees for experts can be astronomical. An attorney of any worth would demand a $100,000 retainer just to get started. And the Funderburk family would have to cough that up times two. They balked at the estimate. They were well off, certainly. But

they weren't prepared to spend that kind of money.
They'd hoped the preliminary hearing would end the
matter. But that kind of thinking, especially in a high-
profile case, was simply naïve. Overwhelmed with the
cost estimates, Jim advised his family to back out and let
the public defender's office take over. Since Matt and Jason had no income of their own, they were entitled to a
county-funded defense.

The decision was a blow to David and his partner
Stephen Klarich. David, especially, had spent a lot of time
with Matt. During visits to prepare for the trial, David
and Matt spent about 20% their time talking about the
case; then the talk always turned to sports, movies, music.
"I always just had the feeling he was a lonely kid,"
David said. "He needed a friend. So I was disappointed
I wouldn't represent him anymore. I became so attached
to Matt. I felt for him. I didn't want to see him go down
for this."

David never saw Matt shed a tear over Jane's death.
But he knew the boy missed her. Even as crazy as she
was, she was the only mother he had ever known. During
one of their last visits together, it was clear Matt was
thinking quite a bit about his mom. He was normally so
reserved. But now, he told David, "She deserved something, but not what she got. She was a bitch, but she
needed to be in an insane asylum."

It soon became clear that Jason was not happy to hear that
a public defender would handle his case. A public defender, he assumed, would be overloaded with cases and
undermotivated to help him. Anyway, weren't all the genuinely talented defense attorneys in private practice, where
the real money is? Not that John Kremer was turning out to

be the Johnnie Cochran of Orange County anyway. But in Jason's mind, a public defender defense carried a stigma he didn't like.

Assistant Public Defender Don Ronaldson ended up with the case. Well into his fifties, Don had been a practicing attorney for nearly thirty years. His experience earned him a team leader position on his office's felony panel (made up of attorneys assigned to handle major cases). Still, Don Ronaldson was not the smoothest attorney in the department. He often looked disheveled, like his hair needed an extra combing, his suit another pressing from the dry cleaner's. He was a nice guy who cared a great deal about his cases. But to onlookers, he appeared to be in over his head. He spoke very little to the reporters who gathered at the various court hearings. "I just don't have time right now" was the usual reply from Ronaldson. From the looks of him, it was true; he appeared overwhelmed.

Matthew would fare better. The public defender's office can't represent more than one client on a case. It's a conflict of interest, since, often, evidence that could clear one client just might convict the other. So attorney Dave Dziejowski, a private practice attorney paid by the county to handle conflict cases, would defend Matt. By his own admission, Dziejowski was not the most experienced trial attorney. But he had worked on plenty of homicide cases, two of them going before a jury. And he was no stranger to major felony cases, having defended gang crimes, rapes, attempted murders, and sexual assaults. He was not married. He had no kids. But he had a huge heart. And as he glanced over Matthew's case, he knew what would help this kid. But there was going to be one major hurdle. He knew Matt and Jason must be very close brothers.

Two kids couldn't grow up in a house like that without learning to lean on each other. But as Dziejowski saw it, if Matt was going to escape a murder conviction, it meant testifying against Jason.

Dave first met Matthew in the juvenile section of the Santa Ana Jail in July 2003. It's where the county held their more serious child offenders, away from the misdemeanor violators in the county's juvenile hall facility. It was only days after Matt's sixteenth birthday. If he were on the outside, he'd be enrolling in driver's education and angling to get his license. Instead, he sat solemnly in front of his new attorney. Dave thought he looked lost.

"He was shell-shocked, I think," said Dave. "I could tell he wanted to talk to me, but he didn't know what to say or how to say it."

Dave wanted desperately to win his new client's trust. He needed that before he could talk to him about turning on Jason. He recognized the psychological toll that losing his last attorney had probably taken on Matt. He hadn't just lost his court ally, he'd lost a friend. Here was a kid who hadn't had many reliable adults in his life, teaching him to trust again would take time.

"I'm going to help you through this," Dave told him. "That's my job. Your brother has his own attorney. I'm sure you care about him. But I'm not here to represent your brother. I'm here to represent you. It's not you alone against the world, okay?"

Matt didn't know what to say, really, but Dave thought he was making headway with the boy.

"So," Dave continued, "I'm going to read through the police reports and get caught up, then I'll come back and we'll talk about the case a little more. Today, I just want to introduce myself."

Jason and Matt lingered in jail for more than a year awaiting trial. Matt was set to go before a jury in October 2004, Jason a few months later, in January 2005.

A few months before trial, Dave Dziejowski sent Mike Murray an email: "Would information about what Jason may or may not have said prior to the killing be helpful?"

Mike read the email. Interesting, he thought. He responded: "Maybe. Let's talk."

Mike would make no promises about cutting a deal with Matthew. He didn't want Matt talking just because there was some offer on the table. He'd listen first, then consider an offer, if Matt said anything worthwhile.

Frankly, the case against Matt had problems, anyway. The most solid evidence Mike had that Matt had known the murder was going to happen came from a teenage friend, Robert Larrermore, who remembered Matt saying that his mom had gone to Chicago in early January. But Larrermore's memory on the timing of that statement was shaky. Sure, there was Matt's confession to dumping the corpse, but jurors could wind up feeling sorry for him and decide that wasn't enough to send him to prison for life. Mike planned on gambling, forcing them to choose between a murder conviction and letting him walk. He didn't file an accessory after the fact charge, knowing the jury might settle on that as a compromise verdict.

Meanwhile, Dave had his own problems. He got his wish, in that Matt finally came to trust him. But with the trial just weeks away, Matt still was not ready to testify against Jason. In late July 2004, Dave sat with Matt again, hoping to get a commitment now that Mike had agreed to listen.

"Look, I understand how you feel," Dave told him. "I had brothers myself. I'm the youngest of seven, you know. And I loved my brothers very much."

"I just don't know if I can do it," Matt said.

"You've got to think about what happened," Dave said. "Think about the situation you're in and who put you in that situation."

Matt knew it was true. If not for Jason, Matt would be nearing his senior year in high school, planning for college, and a life on his own. Now, he faced a potential 25-years-to-life sentence in adult prison. He didn't have a lot of options.

"Just because you testify against Jason doesn't mean you don't love him anymore," Dave said gently. "And, Matt, the outcome could be the same anyway. Jason could very well get convicted with or without your testimony. So don't waste this opportunity to get yourself out from under these charges."

"I want to think about it," Matt said. "Just let me think."

"Okay, think," Dave told him. "But our time is running out."

In August, Dave called Mike Murray.

"Matt's ready," he said. "He wants to talk to you."

"Fine. But, Dave," Mike said, "no promises. I'll sit down with him and just listen. Even if it's helpful to us, I can't promise I'll do anything. But I won't use anything he says against him."

"Fair enough," Dave said.

Three weeks later, the group gathered inside an interview room at the Santa Ana Jail. Mike drew up an agreement granting Matt immunity for this discussion only.

The prosecutor sat with Craig Johnson and Andre Spencer, who would do most of the questioning. Matt sat beside Dave Dziejowski.

"You wanted to talk to us," Andre said. "What about?"

"Well, you know, just that Jason talked about killing Mom before," Matt said. Nothing more.

"And . . . ?" Andre encouraged. "What else?"

"No, I mean, that's mostly it. I just knew it was going to go down, because Jason told me about it before."

"Uh-huh, I see," Andre said.

Mike broke in. Clearly Matt had details to share. But he was being overly vague. Mike didn't know if that was because he didn't want to talk, or because he was just a 15-year-old kid and didn't know what to say. So Mike gave him some not-so-gentle encouragement. "Listen, that's not going to cut it," he said. "We need details. You need to go through this step by step and tell us what happened, got it?"

"Like when did he first tell you he wanted to kill his mom? And how many times?" Andre said.

Matt exhaled a deep breath, and then slouched back in his chair, his arm draped casually over the back. He settled in for the grilling. In the end, he told them everything he knew about Jason's plan to kill their mother. Mike thought Matt's demeanor was so odd—here he was, saying things that would seal his brother's fate, but, just like when he talked about gripping the sleeping bag that had held his mom's remains, he showed no emotion at all.

The observation made Mike realize something. "This is a twisted kid," he said later. "I used to think if your brother says he's going to kill your mom, you do one of two things: you help him or you find a way to stop him. No way do you sit watching TV in the next room, turning up the volume while it all happened. Now, I can see that happening. He's a twisted kid."

25

On January 18, 2005, nearly three years exactly since Jane's murder, Mike Murray stood before jurists. The eleven-woman, one-man jury had no idea what the case was all about. They waited anxiously to hear what this confident, poised prosecutor had to say about the young man seated at the defense table behind him. They had to have noticed Jason, looking sharp in a tan tweed jacket, his thick black-rimmed glasses sitting high on his nose. He looked geeky, as always, except for his haircut—nearly totally shaven from his ears down, and a closely cropped mop of black hair on top. The style was harsh, giving him a bit of a rebel appearance. But for the most part, he looked like a big nerd, not a killer.

"We are here this morning because Jane Bautista was murdered," Mike said. "And she was murdered by her own son, Jason Bautista." At the mention of Jason's name, Mike pointed at the young defendant, staring stoically straight ahead.

"On January fourteenth, 2003, Jason murdered his mother and dumped her like trash. He wrapped his hands around her neck and manually strangled her. And she was beaten. She was beaten so badly, she had fractures to her eye orbits. After the beating, her first-born son decapitated her in the bathtub of her own apartment. Then he cut off her hands."

As he spoke, Mike stood next to a large television. A crime-scene photo filled the screen, one that highlighted that steep, weed-covered ravine along the Ortega Highway. Jane's headless, handless body lay visible at the bottom slope. He told jurors of the investigation that had led them to Jason's school, where he had spun a set of lies for detectives.

"Jason Bautista calmly and coolly tried to manipulate the officers," Mike said. "He said Jane was at a boyfriend's. He said she was out driving around in a Honda. But Jane Bautista was at the bottom of a hill. Then he tells police she has a different appearance—that she's petite and has tattoos, and gives a detailed description of the sunburst on her back and Chinese characters on her body. A complete fabrication, all of it."

Jason had even lied about his relationship with his mom, Mike told them.

"How does he get along with her? He loves his mother, he says. But evidence will show that couldn't be farther from the truth. He hated her. He despised her.

"By the way, as all of this is going on, as investigators are talking to him, Jane Bautista's head and hands are in a closet in his apartment, where he continued to live there with his brother."

A gruesome picture of the black bag holding Jane's head and hands lit up the court TV screen. An older female juror closed her eyes and bowed her head. Jason kept his gaze forward, watching nothing in particular.

"Why does he do all of this? Why does he do something so incomprehensible to most of us? Because Jane Bautista was mentally ill. And Jason didn't like his mother's mental illness. She was difficult, she was volatile. And he *hated* her for it."

Mike laid out the witness list, including classmate William Shadrick and co-workers Crystal Cantu, Kenneth Poarch, and Sarah Reinelt. Then he made the announcement that had to hurt the most.

"And you will hear from Matthew Montejo," Mike said. Jason showed no reaction. He actually had already heard from his attorney that this was coming. But now, to hear it out loud, on the record in court, Jason had to feel the announcement like a punch in the gut. The little brother he'd thought of like a son, the one he'd sworn to protect, had cut a deal with prosecutors. Little Matt would deliver the testimony that would shatter his story of self-defense.

"In short, there is no self-defense in this case," Mike said. "You may hear evidence trying to suggest otherwise, but there is no truth to it. Jason is arrested without a scratch on him, while Jane Bautista was brutally beaten. Then Jason manually strangled the woman who brought him into this world. And he did it because she was mentally ill. And that upset the applecart of his life."

Finally, Mike flashed a picture of Jane's mutilated corpse and pointed dramatically to the screen. "Hold this defendant responsible for what he did to this woman."

He spoke for over an hour before taking his seat next to Andre at the prosecution table and turning the floor to Don Ronaldson. It would be a tough act to follow. Jurors sat rapt as Mike had spoken, spinning the tale of a boy who'd hated his mentally ill mommy so much that he'd rather have chopped off her head than find her help.

Mike exuded confidence in a way that easily earned him the respect and trust of jurors. And while it shouldn't matter, it didn't hurt that he cut a strikingly handsome picture, his young, rugged face easily lifting into a smile

that was infectious, or twisting into dark sarcasm to make
a point. He wore his black hair short and spiky and it was
peppered with just enough gray to give him credibility.
By the end of his opening statement, jurors liked Mike.
And that always helps.

Don Ronaldson's approach was much softer. He was
like an aging father standing there to defend his wayward
child. He looked a little nervous. A strong cowlick made
several strands of his graying hair stand partially erect.

"I am humbled by this case," Don said. "There is nothing in my background to help me understand the dynamics
at work in this family. But if you look at all the investigation work here, things clearly don't add up."

Next to the television screen Mike had used for his
computerized PowerPoint opening, Don set up a large
posterboard and pulled out a packet of stickers. The board
laid out Jane's family tree, and as Don mentioned each
family member, he placed a sticker by their name. He
kept interrupting himself to ask jurors, "Can you see
okay? Can you hear okay?" Every time, jurors nodded
that everything was fine. It had the effect of slowing his
own momentum. It took some time before, eventually, he
got to the point.

"Jane Bautista exhibited bizarre behavior," said Don, explaining how an expert would testify that she was likely a
paranoid schizophrenic.

He focused on the delusions that had caused her to
move multiple times, left her living out of hotels and cars,
and the temper that had sent Jason to the emergency room
with a gash to the head.

"Mr. Murray painted Jason as a cold-hearted murderer,"
Don said. "But there will be testimony presented showing
physical abuse that was criminal. And it went on from the

time he was an infant into adulthood. Evidence will show
she taunted him, she beat him with sticks and clubs and
belts, threatened him with a knife. She hated how he reminded her of Armando, the man who abandoned her by
committing suicide.

"Matt and Jason grew up in an atmosphere of chaos
and insanity. He grew up in a home more desperate, more
psychotic, more poisonous than anyone should have to
bear. And as a result, he developed a defense mechanism
so strong, he could survive in the midst of chaos. In fact,
Matt thought Jason was 'a pussy' for taking so much of
his mom's abuse. He never saw Jason strike back. Never.

"On January fourteenth, 2003, Jane's insanity grew
worse, as it always did around Christmas time. She talked
about Jews and Mexicans. And Jason will testify that his
mother came at him with a knife that night. He feared for
his life. He felt fear like never before, because he saw a
rage in her like he'd never seen before. Jason never intended to kill his mom. But she attacked him, there was a
struggle, and she was dead. This was a struggle, not a
planned killing.

"He did try to cover up. He relied on a TV script for a
half-baked plan. It was a solution so ill-formed and poorly
thought out, he didn't even know what to do with the head
and hands."

Finally, Don turned to the topic of Matt, leaving jurors
with a warning: "Remember, Matthew Montejo was facing life in prison when he made a deal to testify against his
brother. The evidence will show he has a motive to lie and,
therefore, anything he says is unreliable."

With testimony set to begin, reporters from all over
Southern California filled the courtroom. Jim Funderburk

and his wife were there, too. As a future witness, Nellie was barred from the courtroom. That's a standard rule, so that a witness can't be tainted by the testimony of other witnesses. Reporters clamored to get a statement from Jim, who had said nothing publicly since Jason's arrest. "We support him," he said simply.

Sergeant Bill Vining testified first, recounting the memory of Jane's body being pulled up the hillside off the Ortega Highway. "You could see both hands were gone, severed at the wrist joints. And the head was gone, severed at the point just as the neck meets the torso."

Peter Martinez recounted his run-in with the boys outside the Dumpster in Oceanside. Andre Spencer followed, detailing his investigation leading to Jason's arrest, then playing the first taped interview with the defendant, the one filled with tales of Jane running off with an Internet boyfriend, which ended with Jason's cell call urging Matt to run.

But some of the most damaging testimony of the day came from Dr. Richard Fukamoto, chief forensic pathologist with the Orange County Coroner's Office. Fukamoto, a man with so much experience in his field he couldn't even recall how many autopsies he'd performed in his lifetime.

"I quit counting after fifteen thousand," he said.

According to Dr. Fukamoto, Jane had had four blows to the head. "All consistent with delivery by a fist," he said. She had three more across her body, two others to the shoulder. And around her eyes, the bones were deeply fractured. "It's kind of shattered," Fukamoto said. "I could actually just pick the bones apart."

In sum, Jane wasn't just knocked down, or knocked out, she was beaten, nearly to death.

Finally, Dr. Fukamoto explained the bruises covering

Jane's neck, including one that was the perfect impression of a finger. Jane's neck had been squeezed so fiercely, the blood vessels around her eyes, in her eyelids, and above the neck had burst, and blood had seeped into her lungs—all tell-tale signs of a strangulation death.

"And how long does it take for someone to die from strangulation?" Mike asked.

"It takes about three minutes for someone to lose consciousness and appear dead. And it takes about six minutes for the person to die without oxygen," the coroner answered. For six minutes, Jason had held his mother's throat, waiting for her to stop struggling, then waiting for her to die.

A day later, Mike called a Riverside neighbor of the boys to the stand. It must have seemed odd to Jason, since he'd never spoken to Stephen Perotte. But Stephen remembered Jane and her family.

"I remember seeing them walk through the complex," Stephen said. "It was always Jason in front, then Matthew, then her, in that order."

"Did you ever speak to Jane?" Mike asked.

"No, I never spoke to her or Jason, but I exchanged a few hellos with Matt."

"What do you recall about Jane?"

"I saw her with bruises on her face," Stephen said. "She put on sunglasses when I saw her, trying to hide her face."

During the break, a local newspaper reporter asked Mike what the neighbor's testimony was supposed to show.

"I think it was a dry run," Mike said. "I don't think that night was the first time he went after Jane. I think he tried to do it at least once before, but, for whatever reason, he couldn't go through with it then."

26

Mike made his way through a lengthy witness list—nineteen people in all, including investigators, friends privy to Jason's hatred for Jane, and everyone who remembered him mentioning his mom's supposed Chicago plans. William Shadrick even told jurors about the "BADA BING!" sticker Jason had stuck on the Intrigue, and the song lyric his lab partner said he couldn't stop singing.

Finally, on the afternoon of January 19, Mike made the announcement: "The people call Matthew Montejo to the stand."

A sheriff's deputy escorted Matthew to the witness box. He was now 17 years old and still an inmate. Crossing the courtroom, Matthew pointedly avoided Jason's gaze, even though the elder brother broke into a huge smile at the sight of his young sibling. It was a strange reaction, given what Matthew was about to do. But maybe Jason was still holding out hope that Matthew wouldn't tell them everything.

Matthew looked thin and pale as he took the stand. Attorney Dave Dziejowski placed a chair near the witness box and sat next to his client.

"Are you currently charged with a crime?" Mike asked.

"Yes, with murder," Matthew said.

"And while in custody, in September 2004, your attorney contacted me to say you wanted to make a statement, correct?"

"Yes."

"Whose idea was that?"

"My own," Matt said.

"Why did you want to talk?" Mike questioned.

"To have the truth come out."

"And did we enter into an agreement to reduce your charges to accessory after the fact for your cooperation here, and that you would go back to juvenile court to be tried?"

"Yes."

So that was the deal—Matthew would be tried as a juvenile on a reduced charge. Likely he'd be sentenced to no more than 3 years for his part in the crime. Since he'd already served more than 2 years, it was possible a juvenile court judge could parole him any time.

"Matthew, describe what life was like around the end of 2002," Mike prompted.

"We just moved around from place to place. We moved every day. It was a difficult time for the whole family," he said.

Jason, most of all, hated life then, Matt said. "I think it was December 2002 when he made a statement that he wanted to kill her, pretty much. He said things would get better if that happened. That's all he said. The situation calmed down after that."

"How did things calm down?" Mike asked.

"They just got more stable," Matt said. "We were living in a motel for a month or two. Then Jason's financial aid came in, so we had some cash."

By early summer, Jane allowed the family to move into the Riverside apartment, and things were better than ever, Matt said.

"But eventually there was talk of leaving that apartment?"

"Yes, about a month or two before January 2003," Matt said.

"How did your brother react?"

"He didn't like it," Matt said. "We didn't like it. We were both upset."

"In about October or November of 2002, did your brother make another statement about killing?"

"Yes," Matt confirmed. "He said that he wanted to kill her. The situation was getting worse. The house was getting more chaotic, screaming, yelling, she was more paranoid."

"What did he say?" Mike asked.

"He said he wanted to bait her, to get her mad, get her heated," Matt said. "He motioned a chokehold."

"Did he ask for your help?"

"Yes, he wanted me to hold her down, because he said she was pretty strong. But I said, 'No, that's your thing.'"

"Why did he say he wanted to kill her?" Mike asked.

"He said he couldn't move again. He said that would mess things up for him. He needed a stable environment to work and study, and moving would be too much stress for him."

"Did you know your mom was mentally ill?"

"Yes, we both thought she was crazy," Matt said.

On the night of the murder, as Jane began her conspiracy rant, Jason had made a point of calling her crazy, Matt said.

"He normally never does that. He's only ever done that once or twice before."

"And what did she do?" Mike asked.

"She raised her voice higher and said he was part of it, part of the conspiracy."

He recounted the argument, up until he'd gone into his mom's room searching for the dog to play with.

"What made you go into the bathroom?" Mike asked.

"I've heard this stuff for years and I was sick of it," Matt said. "After about twenty minutes, I heard a thud."

"Did you get up to see what just happened?"

"No, I just kept watching TV," Matt said. "I figured either she left or something happened that I didn't really care about. And I didn't want to take care of it."

"So you didn't even care what might have been happening out there?"

"No," he told Mike. "I was into my TV show."

"You just didn't care?" Mike asked again, still incredulous at the thought.

"After multiple years of it, you learn to just zone out."

Hours later, he was in the Intrigue, riding somewhere to help Jason "dump something."

"Do you have any idea what?"

"I figured out what it was," said Matt, mainly because the trunk seemed so heavy. "The whole car was riding different. It had a tilt to it."

It wasn't until the next day, Matt said, that he learned his mom's head and hands were in the hall closet, when Jason forbade him from going in there.

"Did that disturb you, your mother's head and hands in the hall closet?" Mike asked.

"In a way, yes," he said.

"But in a way, no?"

"Not no, but, I just tried to block it out," he said. Still, he couldn't help himself. Curiosity got the best of him and he peeked in the closet "just to see." He found the black zippered bag, but decided against opening it.

Then came the key question, the cornerstone to Jason's defense.

"Matt, did Jason ever tell you Jane attacked him that night?"

"No," Matt said. "He didn't."

"Did he say she came after him with a knife?"

"No."

"Did he look hurt? Was he bleeding anywhere?"

"No."

Matt's tone throughout the entire interview was flat, matter-of-fact. He never cried, he never got mad, he never stuttered. It's the way he'd grown to deal with all the chaos in his life—with a kind of resigned acceptance.

"Matt, why did you wait so long to tell your story?" Mike asked. "Why did you try to lie to investigators?"

"I'm not very fond of police."

"But why?"

"They never did anything for us when we were in our tough situation," said Matt, referring to all the times police came to his house and witnessed their mom's crazy behavior, but did nothing, leaving the boys alone to deal with her.

In cross, Don emphasized Matt's obvious motive to testify against Jason.

"You were hoping for a reduction in your sentence when you met with [the prosecutor], isn't that true?" Don asked.

"Yes, I was weighing my options," he said frankly.

"And you knew you needed to offer something to the prosecutor to get a deal, right?"

"In essence, yes."

"What's going to happen to you now?"

"I'll go home in a couple of weeks," he said.

Of course, jurors would ultimately have to decide whether Matt had lied to get his deal. A ticket out of a life sentence certainly was a powerful motivator. But was it enough to betray the brother who'd cared for him his entire life?

During a court break, Jason and Matt returned to the court's holding cell area, though in separate birdhouses (slang for the court's one-man cages). Still, Matt knew his brother was there, less than twenty feet away and within shouting distance.

"Jason!" he called out. "Jason!"

Jason kept silent, but Matt continued, desperate to get his brother's attention.

"Jason!" he called repeatedly.

Eventually, Jason answered. "Matt, I hear you," he said.

"Jason!" Matt said. "Hey, dude, how's Orange County Jail?"

Matt had nothing important to say to Jason. He just wanted to make the connection, probably hoping to make sure his big brother didn't hate him. They talked for several minutes, shouting back and forth about a favorite computer game, Counter-Strike, and the latest issue of *Rolling Stone* magazine. But Jason had issues on his mind.

"Hey, Matt. Do they know what you're doing?" he said, referring to his fellow inmates. "Do you know what happens to snitches over there?"

The comment filtered through the air, loud enough for all the inmates to hear.

Mike heard about the conversation. Sheriff's deputies

babysitting the custodies told him about it. The prosecutor was furious. Once again, Mike thought, Jason was trying to manipulate the situation, doing his best to intimidate Matthew. When Matt retook the stand, Mike made him recount the conversation. He wanted the jury to glimpse Jason's callousness for themselves. Despite all his talk of caring about his brother, of being like a father figure to him, in the end, he was willing to put him in harm's way.

"Is it bad to be known as a snitch where you're at?" Mike asked.

"Yes."

"Are you afraid now to go back to your cell?"

"In a way, yes. Bad things happen to snitches."

Just to be safe, Dave Dziejowski, Matt's attorney, asked for a new housing assignment. Matt needed all the protection he could get until Dave got him into juvenile court, where he'd plead for his release.

27

Jason's defense case began on January 24, 2005. Matt remained on the stand, this time testifying for his brother by confirming the abuse they'd both endured as Jane slipped deeper into madness. But he didn't testify for long.

"Defense calls Nellie Osborne," Don Ronaldson said.

Jane's mom took the stand looking every bit like a well-manicured lady. She had bright red hair, just like Jane, which she wore cut above the chin. She had on a crisp, white shirt under a navy blazer and a knee-length jeans skirt. Daughter Debbie Cagle had escorted her mom to court that day. She watched now as the clerk swore her in. Nellie spelled her name for the record, but she spoke very slowly, her speech slightly slurred. Last year, she had suffered a stroke. It had been a rough time for so long, she said. First her dad's death, then Jane's, then the boys' arrest. And on August 7, 2004, her mother, Charlie Mae, had passed away.

Nellie testified to the beating she'd taken from Jane in 1980, when she wouldn't let her then–college-age daughter take the car out for the night. "She just attacked me. She hit my eye, my head, my stomach. I tried defending myself. I was trying to hold her. I ended up in the hospital that night."

Nellie knew that her mother had sent checks to Jane

for years. After Charlie Mae had become homebound, Nellie was the one who sent the checks by certified mail to the post office box each month.

On cross, Mike wanted to know if Nellie understood Jane's desperate mental state.

"When you saw her during a Christmas visit back in 1999, was Jane's condition worse?" he asked.

"Truthfully, yes," she said, tears welling in her eyes.

"Were you worried?"

"My grandsons were worries for me," she said. But she never explained why she hadn't interceded.

During a break in court, Mike seemed disturbed by Nellie's testimony. He still couldn't understand why nobody had ever tried to get Jane help. Jason may have killed her, but as Mike saw it, there were a lot of people to blame for her death.

"It bothers me that family knew she was sick," Mike said. "They knew and left those kids with her anyway, just taking care of it by shipping off a monthly check. They had a moral responsibility to that woman, even if it meant involuntary commitment. If I could find a way under the law to hold them legally responsible for what happened, I'd charge them, too."

Dr. Ernest Williams, a psychiatrist specializing in why people commit crimes, testified that after reviewing interviews with Jane's friends and family, he believed she'd suffered from paranoid schizophrenia and a second handicap called narcissistic personality disorder (a sickness that causes the sufferer to believe they're overly important, yet underappreciated, and makes them incapable of sympathizing with others).

Another doctor testified that growing up under such a

woman so scarred Jason that he now suffered from post-traumatic stress disorder.

But in all, the defense spent less than an hour trying to demonstrate the psychological dynamics at work in the Bautista household. Outsiders thought for sure expert testimony would be the cornerstone to Jason's defense, focusing on how years of abuse might have impacted his ability to think reasonably and make decisions rationally, like opting to kill his mother instead of moving away from home. But in truth, such expert testimony was practically a footnote. Before the trial began, Don had asked Judge Frank Fasel to allow additional expert testimony regarding the effects of child abuse. But Fasel ruled such evidence was irrelevant for a 20-year-old murder defendant.

Instead, the most dramatic witness in the defense case would be Jason himself.

It's always a risk putting defendants on the stand. True, it gives them an opportunity to tell their side of the story. But it also leaves them open to the verbal beating a skilled prosecutor can no doubt deliver in cross-examinations. But Don probably had little choice. Cocky, self-assured Jason Bautista likely insisted he testify.

Jason looked every bit the biochemistry student as he took the stand, appearing young and studious in his blue blazer, blue-and-white–checkered shirt, and khaki pants. His skin was ghostly pale, the result of twenty-four months behind bars.

Don Ronaldson wasted no time asking Jason to describe the murder. Only Jason knew what had really happened that night. Now, it was up to him to sell his story of self-defense.

His tale began just like Matt's. Jane was on a rampage. "About the entertainment industry, Mexicans, Isralis, because she supported Palestinian rights, President Clinton, Al Gore. Anybody you see in the newspapers, they were following us and were against us."

"Did she yell at you?" Don asked.

"My entire life."

"About what?"

"My grades weren't good enough, why aren't I in the house more, who is in the conspiracy, who paid me off?" Jason said.

As the fight escalated, "Matt left for the north bedroom," he said.

In the audience, several reporters exchanged glances. "North bedroom?" one said. "Who talks like that? He sounds rehearsed."

Jason said he decided he'd had enough; if she wanted him out, he'd go—but not without the Intrigue.

"I thought it might help me move if I had the Intrigue. I went to look for the keys. Matthew was still in the north bedroom. That's when she went into the kitchen drawer and pulled out her favorite knife," he said.

"A knife," Don repeated.

"Her *favorite* knife," Jason emphasized. Again, he sounded rehearsed. Way too over the top.

"What a disaster," an observer whispered. "He shouldn't be up there."

Don continued: "So you've seen that knife before?"

"Oh, yes. Whenever she threatened us, she'd use that knife. She said, 'You aren't going to leave me like your father did! I made you and I'll destroy you.' So I backed up and sidled away from her."

"Were you afraid?"

"I've always been afraid of her."

"And that night?"

"Extraordinarily," Jason said. "I had a high level of fear that she was going to kill me."

It wasn't just what Jason was saying that rang untrue. It was his delivery. Like a C-rate actor with memorized lines, trying to win a bit part. He was robotic and unemotional. He used technical terms, legal phrases. It was hard to remember that he was talking about his mother's murder.

"What did you do when she came after you with the knife?"

"I stepped back and she came after me, into the living room. She had her grimace face on," Jason said.

"Have you ever resisted her before?"

"Never," Jason said. "I never fought back."

"This time, you did?"

"I tackled her," Jason said. "She stabbed at me with the knife. But she didn't hit me. I moved away and came behind her. I wanted to disarm her."

"Why didn't you just run away, Jason?" Don asked.

"There was nowhere to run. The door was locked and it was such a small apartment. There was nowhere to go."

"What happened next?"

"She said, 'I'm going to kill you!' She was on her knees and I pushed her down onto her stomach."

They struggled on the floor for a long time, Jason said, mostly because he was afraid to stand up, afraid to let her go. He thought she might attack again, Jason said. Then he turned his head, looking directly at the jury, before telling them emphatically, "I was just holding her."

"Where was your arm, Jason?"

"My left arm was around her neck the whole time we were on the ground."

"But at some point, did the struggle cease?" Don asked.

"Yes. I continued to hold her for maybe two minutes

because she was devious. I thought maybe she was playing possum. I grabbed the knife after that and threw it over my shoulder. I didn't know she was dead. I thought she was still playing possum. I made a break for the door. But then I turned around and I see her lying facedown."

"What did you do?" Don said.

"I called out, 'Hey, hey! Are you all right?' "

But Jane didn't move. Jason said he panicked and called out for Matthew. Matthew ran out and checked her pulse. She had none. "And I freaked out."

Jason said he ordered Matt back into Jane's room and then sat down to think. He remembered the *Sopranos* episode and decided that that was the only thing to do— get rid of her body and try to move on with life. He went to the store to buy supplies, then returned. "I moved her body to the vanity area, by South B," he said, referring to the investigators' labeling of the rear bathroom. From there on, Jason said, his memory fails him. "I don't remember what I was thinking," he said. "I just remember thinking, 'I don't want to do this.' "

"Did you love her?"

"Yes," Jason said. "I did."

"But you were afraid of her?" Don questioned.

"All of the time."

"Do you remember cutting off your mother's head?" Don asked.

"No."

"Do you remember cutting off your mother's hands?"

"No."

"Do you remember all the blood in the bathroom?"

"No."

But Mike Murray wasn't going to let Jason get off that easily. His plan was to be very aggressive with him. This was a guy who thought he was smarter than everyone, that he could manipulate his way out of any situation. He could calmly lie under the most stressful of circumstances. So Mike didn't want him to just feel stressed. He wanted him to feel under siege. To do that, Mike showed no mercy.

"Do you remember meeting Andre Spencer on January twenty-fourth, 2003?"

"Well, sir, that whole month seems pretty vague to me," he said.

"Really?" Mike answered. "Because you just gave very detailed testimony about what happened that night."

"Dates and times and things are confusing," Jason said.

"Would it refresh your recollection to hear the taped interview from that day?" Mike asked.

"No, it wouldn't really be beneficial to hear all that testimony. There are a lot of lies," he said.

"Let's talk about lies, then. You lied to Investigator Spencer when you talked to him on January twenty-fourth, 2003?"

"Yes," he said. "I was in denial."

"You were denying to yourself that you murdered your mother?"

"Yes," he said.

"You were denying to yourself that you cut off her head and hands and put them in your closet?"

"Yes," he said again.

"But you weren't in denial enough to lie to protect yourself," said Mike, his voice dripping with sarcasm. "You said, 'My mom's in Corona with her boyfriend. She has, like, a different boyfriend every other week!'"

"Yes, I said that, and yes, that was a lie."

Mike threw other lies in his face: his misleading description of her, her tattoos, her tattoo artist boyfriend, her habit of visiting Internet cafes.

"I don't recall the majority of that day," Jason said.

"You just gave a blow-by-blow, line-by-line dialogue of the night you killed your mother. You repeated line-by-line dialogue with your brother: 'I said this,' 'he said that.' But for some reason, you don't remember this interview?"

"Yes."

"Well, you must have been shocked when you read it."

"Yes, I was."

"Well, it shocks me, too. But let's keep going."

Even the judge wouldn't let Mike go that far. He called for a sidebar and asked him to reel back a touch on the sarcasm. But Mike's approach did have an effect on Jason. He looked nervous, periodically glancing up at the clock above the jurors' heads. Thankfully, it was near the lunch hour and Judge Fasel broke. But over lunch, Mike considered Jason's lack of memory regarding the most gruesome part of his mother's killing. Funny, when he first confessed to investigators, his memory wasn't so foggy. Now, all of a sudden, on the stand, he couldn't talk about it?

As court resumed, Mike asked permission to play back Jason's second interview with detectives. As the tape rolled, jurors heard Jason tell all about Jane's temper, all about her rantings, and all about the murder—including a grisly, detailed account of the decapitation.

"Did you do the wrist first or the head first?" Andre is heard asking.

"I did a wrist first, then the head, then a wrist," Jason said.

"Why did you pick so low on the neck to cut?"

"I just picked a spot that looked good," Jason said.

"Was there a lot of blood?"

"My God. A lot splashed in the room, in the bathroom," he said.

Andre wanted to know how he'd drained his mom of so much blood.

"I just pushed until I thought enough blood came out."

"Was she faceup or facedown?"

"Facedown," Jason said. "And I pushed on it."

After the murder, Jason said, he told Matt, "It will be harder for us. Even though she didn't work, she helped us, she did laundry, she loved us."

The matter-of-fact account flew in the face of Jason's testimony just a few hours ago, claiming not to remember anything. Other details made him look cold—like lamenting over the loss of his favorite gray pants, now soiled with blood, and realizing the arrest meant he'd have to cancel plans for the night: "I was supposed to go hang out with some friends tonight," he'd told Andre. "But I guess I'm not doing that anymore."

As the tape closed, Mike launched his second attack, going over the minute-by-minute version of cutting off each limb, then pushing to drain his mom's blood.

Jason sighed heavily. Remembering everything was tearing him up inside, he said.

"Do you remember telling Investigator Spencer how you ruined your best pair of gray pants?" Mike asked. "Is that one of the things tearing you up inside? Do you remember saying, 'I guess I'm not going out with my friends tonight, jeepers'? Is that one of the things tearing you up inside?"

Finally, Mike zeroed in on Jason's story of the attack.

"So, she comes after you with a knife—'her *favorite*

knife,' " he said mockingly. "And yet you don't even have a nick on you?"

"No," he said.

"Not even a scratch?"

"No."

Mike wanted a description of the struggle, an accounting of whose hand was where and when. Jason, after all, had tried to say the strangling was an accident because he held his mom in a chokehold for too long. But the fingerprint-like bruises around her neck proved otherwise, Mike said. Flustered, Jason said it was too hard to describe every move of the fight.

"Would you like to come down here and demonstrate it on me, then?" Mike asked.

Jason did not, but he had no choice. As he stepped from the witness stand, he turned his back to jurors and faced his attorney. "This is prejudicial," he hissed under his breath. "Object!"

Mike and Andre heard Jason ordering his attorney. They exchanged a glance. It wasn't the first time, either. Throughout the trial, they could hear Jason spit out commands to Don, periodically trying to tell him how to do his job. "Object," he'd say. "You need to object to this!"

In fact, Don did object to the demonstration, calling for a sidebar. But Judge Fasel allowed the re-enactment to go forward, re-creating the struggle with Don. By the end, Jason was on the floor over his attorney in the mock fight, which left Don with a bright red bruise on his forehead. It didn't do much in the way of proving any particular point, but the move clearly rattled Jason, which was exactly what Mike was hoping for.

28

After nine days, the trial drew to a close. In his summation, Mike Murray flashed a series of grisly pictures in front of jurors—the head and hands crammed in the duffel bag, the mutilated and pale corpse. Then he begged them not to believe Jason's "fantastic tale" of self-defense.

"This is a man who can lie, and he lies like most people breathe," he said. "It just comes naturally. It just flows out of his mouth."

And he emphasized that Jason may have grown up with a mentally ill mother, but that was no reason to kill her. "He was a grown man. He was twenty years old. He had options."

Don Ronaldson disagreed, saying Jason had had no choice but to defend himself the night his paranoid schizophrenic mother lunged at him with a knife. He didn't mean to kill her. It just happened. "Was this a murder inspired by a TV show?" he asked. "No. Was there actually a plan? No, there was not."

As the jury spent its third day in deliberations, Mike grew antsy. He'd never had a case out so long. Three days was a long time as jury deliberations go. A day and a half, maybe two days, is the norm for a jury ready to convict. The longer the deliberations, the greater the chances for dissent among jurors. He tried to work on other cases. But every time the phone rang, Mike jumped, hoping for word of a verdict. At times, he gave up pushing the papers around his desk and dropped by the courtroom asking for updates. He chatted amiably with the collection of reporters also waiting for word.

Mike expected a first-degree murder conviction. He'd tolerate second degree, if jurors really didn't buy the premeditation aspect of the case. That would still put Jason away for 15 years to life. But anything less, like manslaughter, which could get Jason as little as 3 years, Mike couldn't stomach. This boy had planned his mom's killing. The jury just had to see that, he thought.

In the jury room, several jurists cried over what they were about to do. As it turned out, two jurors had relatives who suffered from schizophrenia, including one woman's younger brother. The attorneys knew, and each had gambled the experience would come out in their favor. Don thought it would make them empathetic. Mike thought they'd get it—yes, they're hard to live with, but they're sick, not evil.

Jurors took several votes the first two days. Many of them did feel sorry for Jason, enduring such a horrific childhood. Their votes came back all over the map, until Thursday, when it was 11 to 1. One holdout, a woman, wanted to give Jason second-degree murder, nothing more, nothing less. One by one, the 11 jurors took turns explaining why they'd voted as they had.

A juror picked up a plastic skull kept in the jury room for reference purposes and smashed it facedown onto the table, thrashing it left and right. "Do you see this?" the juror said. "Look at this! This is what he did to her!"

Another juror sat silent for most of the deliberations. But now, she broke into tears. "He could have walked away," she said. "And he didn't. He killed her."

By late afternoon on day three, fifteen hours into deliberations, Mike got the call he was waiting for—a verdict.

Jason walked into court wearing his now-familiar blue blazer and tan pants. He glanced at Uncle Jim and smiled, prompting Jim to offer his nephew the thumbs-up sign. Jurors filed in, with one lady visibly gripping a fistful of tissues.

Jason held a stoic look on his face as the verdict was read. On February 4, 2005, jurors pronounced the 22-year-old guilty of first-degree murder. His face was calm, but inside, he was stunned. He'd known he wouldn't get off, but he'd assumed there would be some pity for his story. He'd expected manslaughter, not this.

Jim Funderburk dipped his head in his hands and gently rubbed his forehead. If Jason's face was one of strength, Jim's was one of overwhelming sadness. He grabbed his wife's hand and left court quickly, refusing to talk to reporters. Only Don made a brief statement on Jason's behalf. "Obviously, we are disappointed with the verdict."

Outside of court, 35-year-old juror Lauri Raine paused to explain the verdict. "Jane was beaten beyond anything I've ever seen before in my life," she said angrily. "What happened to Jane Bautista was horrific. We felt very sorry for Jason. We wanted to give him some way out. But in the end, we couldn't."

Juror Patty Clemons, a 34-year-old driver's education teacher and mother of three, had swollen eyes. "Several people have been crying," she said. "This is a young man and we're taking his life away."

Jurors did feel sorry for Jason, who had obviously grown up under challenging conditions. But they also felt sorry for Jane, a woman sinking desperately into madness with nobody, not even her wealthy family, to stretch out a helping hand. She easily could have been murdered, and thrown away, and no one would have ever known what became of her.

"If not for Peter Martinez. And if not for you," Clemons said, calling out to Mike as he stood in the courtroom hallway. "Because of you. You didn't let her death go ignored. You told us, 'Everybody threw Jane away. Don't you do it, too.'"

Mike grinned, slightly embarrassed, slightly basking under the effusive compliment, and acknowledged Andre and Craig. "They prepared the case, I just got to present it. But none of this would have happened without Pete Martinez. He's the hero here. This was a woman with no face to put on TV, no fingerprints. It so easily could have fallen through the cracks."

Interestingly, several jurors told Mike they didn't believe Matt's testimony. "I thought it was all a bunch of lies," Lauri said. "I don't believe he sat in that room watching TV while his mom was dying. Then he just finds out the next day, watching TV, her head was cut off? Come on."

But in the end, Mike said it didn't matter. "There was already so much evidence. Matthew Montejo was just icing on the cake."

As Mike fielded interviews with reporters, Andre stood casually to the side, grinning with relief.

"I just didn't want to see him released," Andre said. "I know the person he is, because I've talked to him. He's a manipulator and he's a liar."

Yes, Jason had grown up in a terrible home, Andre acknowledged. "I feel for him in that sense," he said. "But
thousands of kids grow up in abused households and they
don't kill their parents. So I never forgot who the real victim was here—Jane."

Less than a week later, on February 11, 2005, Matthew sat
before Juvenile Court Judge Robert B. Hutson. "I hope
you have had a chance to reflect on what may have occurred," he said before pleading with him to lead a good
life. "Good luck."

With that, Matt was sentenced to 749 days in jail, the
time he'd already served behind bars, for accessory to
murder after the fact, and then told to go home.

Mike sat across the table from Matt, collecting his
things, as Dave handed the prosecutor an envelope from
his client. Inside was a card that read simply, "Thank you
for giving me a second chance at life."

Wow, Mike thought, there's something in this kid after all.

"He didn't have to do that," Mike said later. "The deal
was done. But in that gesture, I saw a small glimmer of
hope for Matthew. Who knows? At seventeen, I was prepared to screw up my whole life, just because I was seventeen. And Matthew had a lot more pushing against him
to succeed than just being seventeen. He needs counseling, a structured family, and someone there to help him
make a future."

Dave Dziejowski promised Matt he'd be that someone.
Although Matthew was free to go, he didn't have many
places to go to. His family in Illinois had long gone. He
could probably live with them if he asked, Dave thought,
but Matt still considered them strangers. And there were

signs, too, that they were angry with him for testifying against Jason. Throughout the trial, they visited Matt only once, Dave said. But they regularly checked in with Jason.

"They just said, 'We don't want to go over there and make things awkward. We don't want to interfere,'" Dave said. "They were just looking for excuses not to see him."

Instead, Dave drove Matt to San Diego, to his dad's house.

For the past two years, Jose had paid regular visits to both boys in jail. And as it became clearer that Matt would be released, he offered his son a place to stay. It would still be a tough situation. Jose had a temper, too, and the two-some had already had an argument before Matt even made it home.

"I told Matt he couldn't live like Free Willy," Jose said. "He'd have to take responsibility: 'Clean your room, go to school or get a job. Can you handle that?'"

The orders offended Matt, who resented taking them from a man who had been out of his life for so long. He stopped talking to Jose for a few weeks. Then he called.

"Dad," he said. "I may get out of here soon, and I want to come live with you. I understand, I'll live by your rules."

Jose owns his own DJ business, working birthdays, weddings, and baptisms. Matt, who earned his GED in jail, will help Jose run the business now.

As he left court that day, Matt paused in front of Dave's car and just looked up at the sky. He gulped in several deep breaths, then began to laugh.

"Welcome back to the world, my friend," Dave said.

Dave and Matt stopped off for steak before Dave dropped Matt off to his dad. Dave had promised him a steak the day he was freed. And he wanted a man-to-man chat with his newly sprung client.

"You've been in custody for two years," Dave told him. "Those are years you missed out socializing. But your focus needs to be on getting into school, finding some work if you can. Don't be in such a hurry to party and hang out. That stuff will come. But stay focused on what's important—planning a future for yourself."

As he shoved bites of a top sirloin into his mouth, Matt nodded in agreement. "And I'm going to save money, too," he said. "That's the one thing my mom taught me, not to waste money."

"Funny," Dave thought. "He still misses her. He wouldn't talk about her if he didn't."

"Listen, you have demons in your closet," Dave said. "And they'll be there until you address them. You need to address them."

Dave had a psychologist friend in San Diego who agreed to counsel Matt for a greatly reduced rate. Matt agreed to go, but it would be hard to tell if Jose was the kind of dad who would actually make him do it.

"I'm not worried about that," Dave said days after dropping Matt off. "Believe me, he's got people looking out for him, making sure he does what he needs to do. He has me."

29

Jason returned to court one more time on April 8, 2005. It was sentencing day, but even then, he wasn't ready to go down without a fight. He filed a motion in court to fire his attorney and get a new trial.

"I'm not surprised," Mike said when he got the paperwork. "He never got along with his attorney. Right from the starting bell, he was sitting there making faces, gesturing, grumbling at the table."

In a closed court hearing, Jason said his attorney had failed to develop the child abuse angle enough in his case. The way Jason saw it, he suffered from a disease similar to Battered Women's Syndrome, which left abused women so damaged, they feel murder is their only means of escape. True, Don did argue in a pre-trial hearing to allow expert testimony on battered child syndrome. And though it was Judge Fasel who barred the testimony, in part on the grounds that Jason was not a child, Jason blamed his attorney.

Bolstering Jason's claim was the appearance of juror Lauri Raine, the very same juror who'd spoken so passionately outside of court about Jane's beating. Now, she said, she'd changed her mind. "During jury deliberations, I favored a manslaughter verdict up until the point of the coroner's testimony," she said in a brief filed with the court. "I now believe defense expert testimony explaining the impact on Jason being raised by a paranoid schizophrenic mother who physically abused him would have been instrumental in explaining what was in his mind when he killed his mother, and why Jason Bautista remained in the household in the years preceding the killing . . . The absence of this evidence contributed to the jury's verdict."

But Judge Fasel rejected the entire argument and moved swiftly to sentencing. The court opened and reporters filed in, cameramen setting up in the jury box to get their best vantage point. Four deputies lined the small courtroom, just to ensure that nothing went awry. Notably absent this time were Jim Funderburk, his wife, Nellie and Don, and Deborah.

Don, ordered to continue on as Jason's attorney, took a moment to address the court. "This is a killing that stemmed from fear, fear that was instilled in Jason Bautista his entire life." He praised Jason for his hard work, taking on two jobs, going to college, encouraging his brother in school, and avoiding typical college-kid traps like drugs and alcohol. "What he didn't do was seek help. With all due respect to the jury, they didn't take into account his fear."

Judge Fasel listened carefully to Don before turning to look directly at Jason. His words were passionate, forceful. "I think the jury got it exactly right," he said. "This case reeked of premeditation. And you have a total lack of remorse." He chastised Jason for not even taking the time to address the court directly, expressing some sorrow—a typical move for defendants about to be sentenced.

"Do you have anything to say now? Do you want to address the court?"

"Yes, Your Honor," Bautista stuttered, claiming that he had intended to say something all along, but his attorney just hadn't given him the chance.

"Your Honor, I'm very sorry for my actions. I know they were extremely wrong, and I'm very sorry for everything. I don't agree with the first-degree verdict, but, um, I submit," he said. The very brief speech came out in a rush. It sounded so insincere, especially coming after the lengthy pre-written letters of regret read by other defendants sentenced earlier that morning. If anything, the judge sounded more irritated than ever.

"That's it?"

"Yes, I submit," he said.

"Well, I think the jury got it right. And I think the probation officer also got it right," Fasel said. Prior to sentencing, a probation officer interviews each defendant and their families before making a recommendation regarding remorse and punishment. Jason's probation officer had come down hard on him.

In a way, it was Jason's intellect that was his undoing. He spent so much time proving to everyone how smart he was. And he was smart. Way too bright, in fact, not to know how to reach out for help. The probation report echoed as much.

According to the report, which the judge read aloud, "You sought no help from professionals. It's inconceivable the defendant was unaware there were means for dealing with his mother's illness other than resorting to violence. And rather than explore those options, he chose to dismember her body."

After Jane's murder, the report focused on Matt and Jason's playtime. "They invited friends over to the house to play video games. They planned a Super Bowl party.

It's hard to believe he felt any remorse. He is obviously a deeply troubled young man."

Fasel stopped reading and looked again at Jason. "I totally agree," Fasel said. "Based on that, I sentence you to twenty-five years to life. That's the court's order. Do you understand?"

"Yes, Your Honor."

Oddly, after the verdict, Jason leaned over to chat with Don, smiling and laughing as the deputies approached to put him back in cuffs and lead him away.

Outside of court, Mike turned to Andre and had to chuckle. " 'I submit.' Like he's an attorney."

"This entire time," Andre said, "he thought he was a better attorney than Don. But given a chance to have his say, he comes up with two sentences, that's it."

"You know he had nothing planned to say to the judge until he saw how pissed he was at his total lack of remorse," Mike said.

Standing before a camera crew, Mike let his feelings fly. "The jury did get it right. The defendant has no remorse and hasn't from day one. He tried to show some when the judge called him on it, at which point he did what he did since the beginning of this case: he started to dance. But he didn't feel his words, and it showed. Today, he got the verdict he deserves."

Craig and Andre celebrated the conclusion of the case with a Southern-themed lunch of gumbo and corn bread at their favorite greasy spoon restaurant.

As they rehashed it all, they considered how tragic the losses were on so many levels—a mother slain, a son in jail for years, another son scarred for life.

"But you know what's most tragic about the sentencing

today?" Andre asked. "No one was there for Jane. She was the one who was sick, who was murdered, but there was no sympathy from her family, from her kids. There was no one to speak up for Jane, except us."